INSPIRATIONAL
BASKETBALL
SHORT
STORIES
FOR YOUNG READER

CONTENTS

CONTENTS

CONTENTS

INTRODUCTION

Welcome to "Inspirational Stories: 30 Greatest Basketball Players"! This book is a collection of profiles on some of the most talented and inspiring basketball players to ever grace the court. From Michael Jordan to LeBron James, each of these individuals has left a lasting impact on the sport and have inspired millions of fans around the world.

Basketball is more than just a game; it is a way of life for many people. The thrill of the competition, the rush of adrenaline, and the camaraderie of the team all come together to create a unique and exciting experience. But it is the players themselves who truly make the game what it is. These athletes are some of the most dedicated and hard-working people in the world, constantly pushing themselves to be better and to reach their full potential.

In this book, you will read about the journey of some of the greatest basketball players of all time. Each chapter tells the story of a different player, starting with their early days on the court and following them through their careers and accomplishments. You will learn about their struggles and setbacks, as well as their triumphs and achievements. But most importantly, you will see how each of these players used their love for the game to inspire and motivate others.

Whether you are a die-hard basketball fan or simply looking for some inspiration in your own life, "Inspirational Stories: 30 Greatest Basketball Players" has something for everyone. These profiles are not just about the statistics and accomplishments of these athletes, but about the people behind the numbers. Each chapter tells the story of a real person, with their own unique experiences and challenges.

So sit back, relax, and get ready to be inspired by some of the greatest basketball players of all time. From Michael Jordan's iconic slam dunks to LeBron James's clutch performance in the NBA Finals, these stories are sure to captivate and inspire you. Whether you are a seasoned fan or just getting started, there is something for everyone in this collection of profiles on the 30 greatest basketball players of all time.

MICHAEL JORDAN

MICHAEL JORDAN WAS ACTUALLY CUT FROM HIS HIGH SCHOOL BASKETBALL TEAM IN HIS SOPHOMORE YEAR. HE USED THIS AS MOTIVATION TO WORK HARDER AND IMPROVE HIS SKILLS, EVENTUALLY LEADING TO HIS SUCCESS AS A PROFESSIONAL ATHLETE.

JORDAN IS KNOWN FOR HIS FIERCE COMPETITIVE SPIRIT, BUT HE ALSO HAS A SOFTER SIDE. HE HAS DONATED MILLIONS OF DOLLARS TO VARIOUS CHARITIES AND IS INVOLVED IN NUMEROUS PHILANTHROPIC CAUSES.

JORDAN WAS NOT ONLY A SUCCESSFUL BASKETBALL PLAYER, BUT ALSO A SUCCESSFUL BUSINESSMAN. HE HAS ENDORSEMENT DEALS WITH NUMEROUS COMPANIES, INCLUDING NIKE, GATORADE, AND HANES, AND OWNS HIS OWN BRAND, JORDAN BRAND.

IN ADDITION TO BASKETBALL, JORDAN ALSO TRIED HIS HAND AT PROFESSIONAL BASEBALL. HE PLAYED FOR THE CHICAGO WHITE SOX MINOR LEAGUE TEAM IN 1994, BUT ULTIMATELY RETURNED TO BASKETBALL.

JORDAN IS KNOWN FOR HIS INCREDIBLE DUNKING ABILITY, BUT HE ALSO HOLDS THE RECORD FOR THE MOST POINTS SCORED IN A SINGLE NBA GAME, WITH 69 POINTS.

JORDAN HAS A FAMOUS GAMBLING HABIT, WITH RUMORS OF HIM LOSING MILLIONS OF DOLLARS IN VARIOUS CASINO GAMES. HOWEVER, HE HAS ALSO WON BIG, INCLUDING A $1.25 MILLION PAYOUT IN A GOLF TOURNAMENT.

JORDAN HAS A STRONG RELATIONSHIP WITH HIS FAMILY, INCLUDING HIS FIVE CHILDREN AND WIFE, YVETTE PRIETO. HE IS ALSO CLOSE WITH HIS MOTHER, WHO HAS OFTEN ATTENDED HIS GAMES AND SUPPORTED HIS CAREER.

JORDAN IS A PHILANTHROPIST AND HAS DONATED MILLIONS OF DOLLARS TO VARIOUS CHARITIES OVER THE YEARS, INCLUDING THE BOYS AND GIRLS CLUB, THE CHILDREN'S HEALTH FUND, AND THE UNITED NEGRO COLLEGE FUND.

JORDAN HAS A PASSION FOR GOLF AND HAS PLAYED IN NUMEROUS GOLF TOURNAMENTS OVER THE YEARS. HE EVEN HAS HIS OWN PRIVATE GOLF COURSE IN FLORIDA.

DESPITE HIS SUCCESS ON THE COURT, JORDAN HAS STRUGGLED WITH MENTAL HEALTH ISSUES, INCLUDING ANXIETY AND DEPRESSION. HE HAS TALKED OPENLY ABOUT HIS STRUGGLES AND HAS ENCOURAGED OTHERS TO SEEK HELP FOR THEIR OWN MENTAL HEALTH ISSUES.

DID YOU KNOW?

WHO AM I?

Name..

Nickname..

ABOUT ME

Skill

_____

Born

_____

Year Started

_____

INTERESTING FACTS ABOUT ME

1 _____

2 _____

3 _____

Michael Jordan was a man who loved to play basketball. He was tall and strong, with a powerful jump and a fierce determination to win. He was the best basketball player in the world, and he inspired millions of people around the globe with his talent, his hard work, and his never-give-up attitude.

Michael was born in Brooklyn, New York, on February 17, 1963. He was the fourth of five children, and his parents were James and Deloris Jordan. James was a mechanic, and Deloris was a bank teller. Both of them worked hard to provide for their family, and they instilled in their children the importance of education and hard work.

Michael loved sports from a young age. He played basketball, football, and baseball in high school, and he excelled at all of them. He was tall and athletic, with a natural talent for the game. But basketball was his true passion. He loved the feeling of the ball in his hands, the roar of the crowd, and the thrill of competition.

After high school, Michael went on to play college basketball at the University of North Carolina. He led the Tar Heels to a national championship in 1982, and he was named the NCAA College Player of the Year. He was also named to the All-American team three times.

In 1984, Michael was drafted by the Chicago Bulls in the NBA. He quickly became one of the best players in the league, and he led the Bulls to six NBA championships. He was named the NBA's Most Valuable Player five times, and he won numerous other awards and accolades.

But Michael's success on the court was just the beginning. He became a global icon, and he inspired millions of people with his talent, his hard work, and his never-give-up attitude. He endorsed products, appeared in movies and TV shows, and even had his own line of sneakers.

But despite all of his success, Michael never forgot where he came from. He gave back to his community by supporting various charities and foundations, and he encouraged young people to work hard and pursue their dreams.

"I can't accept not trying," he once said. "I have to go out and get what I want. I have to be willing to work hard for it. And I have to be willing to face failure and keep going. That's what it means to be a winner."

Michael Jordan was a true role model, and his story is one of inspiration and perseverance. He showed us that with hard work and determination, anything is possible. He is a shining example of what it means to be a true champion, both on and off the court.

So if you're a young person reading this, remember that you, too, can achieve greatness. Don't be afraid to dream big, and don't be afraid to work hard for what you want. Follow your heart and your passions, and never give up. You never know where your dreams may take you.

LeBron James

LeBron James was born on December 30, 1984 in Akron, Ohio.

He attended St. Vincent-St. Mary High School in Akron, where he was a standout basketball player and was featured on the cover of Sports Illustrated as a high school junior.

LeBron was the first overall pick in the 2003 NBA Draft, chosen by the Cleveland Cavaliers.

He has won four NBA championships, two with the Miami Heat and two with the Cleveland Cavaliers.

LeBron has been named the NBA Finals MVP four times, tying him with Michael Jordan for the most in NBA history.

He has also won four Olympic gold medals, representing Team USA in the 2008, 2012, and 2016 Summer Olympics.

LeBron has been named the NBA Most Valuable Player four times and has been selected to the All-NBA First Team 13 times.

He has also been named to the NBA All-Defensive First Team five times.

In addition to his basketball career, LeBron has also made a name for himself off the court as a philanthropist and business mogul. He has established a number of charitable foundations, including the LeBron James Family Foundation, and has endorsement deals with numerous major brands.

LeBron is also an avid fan of soccer and has been seen wearing soccer jerseys and supporting various soccer clubs around the world. He even owns a small stake in Premier League club Liverpool FC.

DID YOU KNOW?

WHO AM I?

Name..

Nickname..

ABOUT ME

Skill

_____

Born

_____

Year Started

_____

INTERESTING FACTS ABOUT ME

 _____

 _____

 _____

Lebron James is a professional basketball player known for his incredible talent and passion for the game. His determination and dedication to improving his skills have made him one of the greatest players of all time, and his inspiring story is an inspiration to children everywhere.

Born on December 30, 1984, in Akron, Ohio, Lebron was raised by his mother Gloria James and his father Anthony McClelland. From a young age, Lebron showed a natural talent for basketball and spent hours practicing on the court. He joined the varsity basketball team at St. Vincent-St. Mary High School in Akron and quickly became one of the best players in the state.

In 2003, Lebron declared for the NBA draft and was selected first overall by the Cleveland Cavaliers. He made an immediate impact in the league, leading the Cavs to the playoffs in his rookie year and being named Rookie of the Year. Over the next few years, Lebron continued to improve his game, leading the Cavs to the NBA Finals in 2007.

In 2010, Lebron became a free agent and decided to join the Miami Heat. He led the team to four straight NBA Finals appearances and won two championships. In 2014, Lebron returned to the Cleveland Cavaliers and led them to four straight NBA Finals appearances, winning the championship in 2016.

Throughout his career, Lebron has demonstrated incredible leadership, perseverance, and dedication to his craft. He is known for his hard work and dedication to improving his skills, and he has inspired countless young players to follow their dreams and work hard to reach their goals.

One of the things that makes Lebron such an inspiration to children is his commitment to giving back to his community. He has worked with numerous charities and foundations, including the LeBron James Family Foundation, which focuses on improving education and opportunities for children in his hometown of Akron.

Lebron has also used his platform to speak out on social and political issues, including police brutality and racial injustice. He has encouraged young people to get involved in their communities and make a difference in the world.

Lebron's story is an inspiration to children everywhere. It teaches them that hard work, dedication, and perseverance can help them achieve their goals and make a difference in the world. His commitment to giving back to his community and speaking out on important issues is a powerful example of how anyone can make a positive impact on the world.

So if you're a young basketball player looking to improve your skills and reach your goals, remember Lebron's story. Work hard, stay dedicated, and never give up. And always remember to give back to your community and make a difference in the world. With hard work and determination, you too can achieve greatness and make your dreams a reality.

Kobe Bryant

Kobe was the youngest player to ever start an NBA game at 18 years old.

He was a high school dropout and did not attend college.

Kobe was a member of the 1992 United States Olympic basketball team, known as the "Dream Team".

He was a fan of Italian soccer club AC Milan and often wore their jersey during his free time.

Kobe was fluent in Italian and often traveled to Italy during the off-season.

He was named after the famous Japanese beef, Kobe, as his parents were foodies.

Kobe won an Academy Award in 2018 for his short film "Dear Basketball".

He was a huge fan of rap music and even recorded a rap song under the pseudonym "The Black Mamba".

Kobe was a vocal advocate for women's sports and was a strong supporter of the WNBA.

He owned his own production company, Granity Studios, which focused on creating content for young audiences.

DID YOU KNOW?

WHO AM I?

Name..

Nickname..

ABOUT ME

Skill

_____

Born

_____

Year Started

_____

INTERESTING FACTS ABOUT ME

 1 _____

 2 _____

 3 _____

Kobe Bryant was a legendary basketball player who inspired countless children around the world with his passion, dedication, and love for the game. From a young age, Kobe knew that he wanted to be a basketball player, and he worked hard every day to make his dreams a reality.

When Kobe was just six years old, he started playing basketball in his backyard with his father, Joe "Jellybean" Bryant. Joe was a former professional basketball player himself, and he knew exactly what it took to succeed in the game. He taught Kobe everything he knew about basketball, from ball handling and shooting to passing and defense.

As Kobe grew older, he continued to work on his skills, practicing every day after school and on weekends. He was determined to become the best basketball player he could be, and he knew that it would take a lot of hard work and dedication to reach his goals.

Eventually, Kobe's hard work paid off, and he was given the opportunity to play high school basketball at Lower Merion High School in Pennsylvania. It was there that Kobe really began to shine, leading his team to a 31-3 record and earning a spot on the all-state team.K

After high school, Kobe decided to bypass college and go straight to the NBA, where he was drafted by the Charlotte Hornets. However, Kobe's real dream was to play for the Los Angeles Lakers, and he was eventually traded to the team.

It was with the Lakers that Kobe truly made a name for himself, leading the team to five NBA championships and becoming one of the best players in the league. Kobe was known for his incredible scoring ability, as well as his tenacity and determination on the court. He always gave 100% every time he stepped onto the court, and his passion for the game inspired countless children around the world.

But Kobe was more than just a great basketball player; he was also a role model and an inspiration to children everywhere. He always encouraged kids to follow their dreams and to never give up, no matter how hard things might seem. He also stressed the importance of education and working hard in school, and he often visited schools and spoke to children about the importance of education.

Kobe was a true role model for children, and his legacy will live on for generations to come. His love for the game and his dedication to improving himself and inspiring others will always be remembered and celebrated.

So if you're a child who loves basketball, or if you just want to be the best you can be at whatever it is you love to do, remember Kobe Bryant and his inspiring story. Never give up on your dreams, and always work hard to achieve them. With hard work and determination, you can accomplish anything you set your mind to.

Magic Johnson

Magic Johnson was born on August 14, 1959 in Lansing, Michigan.

He attended Everett High School in Lansing, where he led his team to a state championship in 1977.

Johnson was selected first overall in the 1979 NBA Draft by the Los Angeles Lakers.

He was a member of the "Dream Team" that won gold at the 1992 Summer Olympics in Barcelona.

Johnson retired from the NBA in 1991 after announcing that he was HIV-positive.

He returned to the Lakers in 1996 and played 32 games before retiring for good.

In addition to his successful basketball career, Johnson is also a successful businessman and philanthropist.

He owns several Starbucks franchises, a movie theater chain, and is a part-owner of the Los Angeles Dodgers.

Johnson has also been actively involved in HIV/AIDS awareness and prevention efforts.

He was inducted into the Basketball Hall of Fame in 2002.

DID YOU KNOW?

WHO AM I?

Name..

Nickname..

ABOUT ME

Skill

_____

Born

_____

Year Started

_____

INTERESTING FACTS ABOUT ME

 _____

 _____

 _____

Magic Johnson was a basketball player who had an incredible talent for the game. He was born in Lansing, Michigan on August 14, 1959, and from a young age, it was clear that he had a special gift for basketball.

Growing up, Magic played basketball every chance he got. He practiced for hours on end, perfecting his skills and techniques. He was driven and determined to be the best, and his hard work paid off.

In high school, Magic led his team to a state championship, and his impressive performance caught the attention of college recruiters. He decided to attend Michigan State University, where he continued to excel on the court.

During his college career, Magic led the Spartans to a National Championship and was named the Most Outstanding Player of the Final Four. He was also named a First Team All-American, and it was clear that he was destined for greatness.

After college, Magic was drafted by the Los Angeles Lakers, and he quickly became a fan favorite. His enthusiasm and love for the game was contagious, and he quickly became one of the most popular players in the league.

Magic's career was filled with many highlights and accomplishments. He was a five-time NBA champion, a three-time Finals MVP, and a nine-time NBA All-Star. He was also inducted into the Basketball Hall of Fame in 2002.

Despite his many accolades, Magic's biggest accomplishment came off the court. In 1991, he announced that he had been diagnosed with HIV, a virus that can lead to AIDS. At the time, there was a lot of fear and stigma surrounding HIV, and many people believed that Magic's career was over.

But Magic refused to let his diagnosis define him. He continued to play basketball, and even led the Dream Team to a gold medal at the 1992 Olympics. He also became an advocate for HIV awareness, using his platform to educate people about the importance of safe sex and the realities of living with HIV.

Magic's resilience and determination inspired people around the world, and he became a role model for children everywhere. He showed that no matter what challenges you face, you can overcome them with hard work and a positive attitude.

Today, Magic is still an active and influential figure in the world of basketball. He is the owner of the Los Angeles Dodgers, and he remains dedicated to educating people about HIV and promoting safe sex practices.

Magic's story is an inspiration to children everywhere. It teaches them that no matter what obstacles they face, they can overcome them with hard work and a positive attitude. It shows them that they can achieve anything they set their minds to, and that they should never let fear or stigma hold them back.

So if you're a child who loves basketball, or just someone who wants to achieve greatness in life, take a lesson from Magic Johnson. Believe in yourself, work hard, and never give up. With dedication and determination, you too can achieve greatness.

Larry Bird

Larry Bird was born in West Baden Springs, Indiana in 1956.

He played college basketball at Indiana State University and led the team to the NCAA Championship in 1979.

1. Bird was drafted 6th overall by the Boston Celtics in the 1978 NBA Draft.
He won three NBA championships with the Celtics in 1981, 1984, and 1986.

Bird was a five-time NBA MVP and a three-time NBA Finals MVP.

He was also named to the NBA All-Defensive Team twice and made the NBA All-Star Team 12 times.

Bird was inducted into the Naismith Memorial Basketball Hall of Fame in 1998.

In addition to his success on the court, Bird was also known for his trash-talking and competitive nature.

He had a rivalry with fellow NBA great Magic Johnson, which helped to popularize the sport in the 1980s.

Bird was drafted 6th overall by the Boston Celtics in the 1978 NBA Draft.

After retiring from playing, Bird became a coach and led the Indiana Pacers to the NBA Finals in 2000. He has also served as a team president and executive for the Pacers.

DID YOU KNOW?

WHO AM I?

Name..

Nickname..

ABOUT ME

Skill

_____

Born

_____

Year Started

_____

INTERESTING FACTS ABOUT ME

 _____

 _____

 _____

Larry Bird was a basketball player who played for the Boston Celtics in the NBA. He was known for his incredible skill and leadership on the court, and his determination to always give his best effort.

Growing up in rural Indiana, Larry Bird had a love for sports from a young age. He excelled in basketball, and by the time he was in high school, he was already one of the best players in the state. Despite his talent, however, Larry Bird was not highly recruited by college basketball programs. He ended up attending Indiana State University, where he worked hard to improve his game and became one of the best players in the country.

After college, Larry Bird was drafted by the Boston Celtics in the NBA. He quickly became a leader on the team, and his hard work and dedication helped lead the Celtics to three NBA championships. Larry Bird was also a fierce competitor, and he always gave his all on the court. He was known for his incredible shooting ability and his ability to make difficult shots look easy.

Larry Bird was not only a great basketball player, but he was also a role model for children. He always showed respect for his opponents and worked hard to be the best that he could be. He was a true sportsman, and he inspired many young people to work hard and never give up on their dreams.

Despite his many accomplishments on the court, Larry Bird remained humble and gracious. He always gave credit to his teammates and coaches, and he never let success go to his head. He remained focused on the game and always put the team first.

Larry Bird's hard work and dedication to the game of basketball inspired many young people to pursue their own dreams and to never give up. He showed that with determination and hard work, anything is possible. His legacy lives on as a true inspiration to children and athletes everywhere.

Bill Russell

Bill Russell is a retired professional basketball player who played center for the Boston Celtics from 1956 to 1969.

He is considered one of the greatest basketball players of all time, winning 11 NBA championships during his career, the most by any player in NBA history.

Russell was a dominant defensive player, leading the league in rebounds and blocks multiple times throughout his career.

He was the first African American head coach in the NBA, serving as player-coach for the Celtics in 1966.

Russell was the first player in NBA history to win a championship in his rookie season, leading the Celtics to their first title in 1957.

He was named NBA Finals MVP five times, and was inducted into the Naismith Memorial Basketball Hall of Fame in 1975.

In addition to his success on the court, Russell was also a vocal civil rights activist and advocate for social justice.

He was the first African American to win the Sports Illustrated Sportsman of the Year award in 1968.

Russell was also a successful coach, leading the Seattle SuperSonics to the NBA Finals in 1978.

In his later years, he became a successful businessman and television commentator, and was also a vocal critic of the NCAA and its treatment of student athletes.

DID YOU KNOW?

WHO AM I?

Name..

Nickname..

ABOUT ME

Skill

_____

Born

_____

Year Started

_____

INTERESTING FACTS ABOUT ME

 1 _____

 2 _____

 3 _____

Bill Russell was a powerful football player who loved nothing more than running down the field and scoring touchdowns. He had always dreamed of playing in the NFL, and when he finally made it, he became one of the best players in the league.

Bill was a tall, strong, and fast runner who could outmaneuver any defender. He was also a great leader on the field, always encouraging his teammates to give their best effort.

One day, Bill was playing in a big game against the New York Giants. The Giants were known for their tough defense, but Bill was determined to lead his team to victory.

As the game began, the Giants defense was all over the field, trying to stop Bill and his teammates from making any big plays. But Bill was not about to let them stand in his way.

He ran up and down the field, dodging and weaving his way through the Giants defense, making catch after catch and scoring touchdown after touchdown.

The Giants were no match for Bill's speed and strength, and he led his team to a huge victory.

After the game, the crowd went wild, cheering and clapping for their favorite player. Bill was hailed as a hero, and he basked in the glory of his team's victory.

But despite all the accolades, Bill never forgot where he came from. He knew that he had worked hard and earned his success, and he was always grateful for the opportunity to play football.

He continued to work hard and lead his team to victory, becoming one of the most respected and feared players in the NFL.

And even when he retired from football, he remained an inspiration to children all over the world, showing them that with hard work and determination, they could achieve anything they set their minds to.

So if you ever see a young football player running down the field, chasing their dreams and scoring touchdowns, just remember – they might just be the next Bill Russell, a powerful and inspiring athlete who never gave up.

Wilt Chamberlain

Wilt Chamberlain was known for his incredible physical strength and athletic ability, standing at 7 feet 1 inch tall and weighing over 300 pounds.

He was the first player to score 100 points in a single NBA game, a feat that has never been matched.

Chamberlain holds the record for most points scored in a season, with 4,029 points in the 1961-62 season.

He also holds the record for most rebounds in a season, with 2,149 rebounds in the 1960-61 season.

Chamberlain won two NBA championships, one with the Philadelphia 76ers in 1967 and one with the Los Angeles Lakers in 1972.

He was named NBA MVP four times and was named to the All-NBA First Team ten times.

In addition to his success in the NBA, Chamberlain also played professionally in the ABA and was a member of the USA Olympic basketball team in 1964.

Chamberlain was also an avid athlete outside of basketball, participating in track and field events and even trying out for the Olympic decathlon team.

He was known for his philanthropy and charitable work, establishing the Wilt Chamberlain Fund to support education and sports programs for inner city youth.

Chamberlain wrote several books, including a memoir titled "Wilt: Just Like Any Other 7-Foot Black Millionaire Who Lives Next Door," which was published posthumously in 2002.

Wilt Chamberlain

DID YOU KNOW?

WHO AM I?

Name..

Nickname..

ABOUT ME

Skill

_____

Born

_____

Year Started

_____

INTERESTING FACTS ABOUT ME

1 _____

2 _____

3 _____

Wilt Chamberlain was a professional basketball player who played for the Philadelphia 76ers, Los Angeles Lakers, and San Francisco Warriors. He was known for his size and strength, and was one of the most dominant players in the history of the game. But before he became a basketball legend, Wilt was a talented football player.

As a young boy, Wilt was always active and loved playing sports. He was especially skilled at football, and quickly became one of the best players on his school's team. Despite his size and strength, Wilt was also fast and agile, and was able to outmaneuver opponents on the field.

As he grew older, Wilt's football skills continued to improve, and he became a star player in high school. He was recruited by colleges across the country, and ultimately chose to attend the University of Kansas on a football scholarship.

At Kansas, Wilt excelled on the football field, and was a key member of the team. He was known for his hard work and dedication, and was always willing to put in the extra effort to improve his skills.

Despite his success on the football field, Wilt eventually decided to pursue a career in basketball. He knew that he had the size and strength to excel in the sport, and he was determined to become one of the best players in the world.

Through hard work and dedication, Wilt achieved his dream, and became one of the greatest basketball players of all time. He was inducted into the Basketball Hall of Fame in 1978, and his legacy lives on today as an inspiration to young athletes everywhere.

Wilt Chamberlain's story is a reminder that with hard work and determination, anyone can achieve their dreams, no matter how big or seemingly impossible they may seem. So, always be determined and never give up on your dreams.

Shaquille O'Neal

Shaquille O'Neal, also known as Shaq, is a retired American professional basketball player who is widely considered one of the greatest players in the history of the sport.

O'Neal was born on March 6, 1972, in Newark, New Jersey, and grew up in San Antonio, Texas. He played college basketball at Louisiana State University before being drafted by the Orlando Magic with the first overall pick in the 1992 NBA Draft.

O'Neal was a dominant force on the court, standing at 7 feet 1 inch tall and weighing over 300 pounds. He was known for his powerful dunks and dominant post play, and was a four-time NBA champion and three-time NBA Finals MVP.

O'Neal's professional career spanned 19 seasons and included stints with the Orlando Magic, Los Angeles Lakers, Miami Heat, Phoenix Suns, Cleveland Cavaliers, and Boston Celtics.

In addition to his basketball career, O'Neal has also pursued a successful career as a television personality and analyst, and has appeared in a number of movies and television shows.

O'Neal has also been involved in a number of philanthropic efforts, including establishing a scholarship fund for underprivileged students and supporting various children's hospitals.

O'Neal is also known for his rap music career, and released several albums in the 1990s and 2000s.

O'Neal has been married twice and has six children.

O'Neal is an avid collector of classic cars, and has a collection that includes a Lamborghini Murcielago, a Bentley Continental GT, and a Rolls-Royce Phantom.

In 2016, O'Neal was inducted into the Basketball Hall of Fame.

Shaquille O'Neal

DID YOU KNOW?

WHO AM I?

Name..

Nickname..

ABOUT ME

Skill

_____

Born

_____

Year Started

_____

INTERESTING FACTS ABOUT ME

 _____

 _____

 _____

Shaquille O'Neal was a towering presence on the football field. Standing at an impressive 7 feet tall, he was a force to be reckoned with. His massive frame and strength made him a dominant player, and he quickly became one of the most feared defensive linemen in the league.

But Shaquille was more than just a football player. He was a role model and an inspiration to children everywhere. His larger-than-life personality and positive attitude made him a beloved figure, and his hard work and dedication on and off the field made him an example for all young athletes to follow.

One of the things that made Shaquille such a great role model was his commitment to education. Despite being a star athlete, he always made time for his studies and earned his degree in criminal justice. He understood the importance of education and worked hard to set a good example for kids everywhere.

Shaquille was also known for his charitable work. He was always looking for ways to give back to his community and help those in need. Whether it was visiting sick children in the hospital or donating money to various charities, Shaquille was always willing to lend a helping hand.

But perhaps the most inspiring thing about Shaquille was his determination and perseverance. He faced many challenges throughout his career, but he never let them hold him back. He always worked hard and never gave up, and that perseverance paid off in the end.

One of the most memorable moments of Shaquille's career came in the Super Bowl. He had always dreamed of winning the championship, and he finally got his chance when his team made it to the big game. The pressure was on, but Shaquille didn't let it get to him. He played his heart out and helped lead his team to victory, earning the coveted Super Bowl ring.

For kids everywhere, Shaquille O'Neal's story is one of determination, hard work, and perseverance. His dedication to his craft and his commitment to making a difference in the world make him a role model to be admired and emulated. He is proof that with hard work and determination, anyone can achieve their dreams.

Shaquille's journey wasn't always easy, but he never let that stop him. He faced challenges and setbacks along the way, but he always got back up and kept fighting. He knew that with hard work and determination, he could overcome any obstacle.

For young athletes, Shaquille's story is a reminder that with hard work and perseverance, anything is possible. Whether you're on the football field or in the classroom, you can achieve your dreams if you set your mind to it and never give up.

So take a lesson from Shaquille O'Neal, and remember that with hard work and determination, you can accomplish anything you set your mind to. Keep pushing forward, never give up, and you too can achieve greatness.

Kareem Abdul-Jabbar

Kareem Abdul-Jabbar, also known as Lew Alcindor, was born on April 16, 1947 in New York City.

He was a dominant center in the NBA, playing for the Milwaukee Bucks and the Los Angeles Lakers.

Abdul-Jabbar was a six-time NBA champion and a six-time NBA Most Valuable Player.

He holds the record for the most points scored in NBA history, with 38,387.

Abdul-Jabbar was a member of the United States men's Olympic basketball team that won gold medals at the 1968 and 1972 Summer Olympics.

He was inducted into the Naismith Memorial Basketball Hall of Fame in 1995.

In addition to his basketball career, Abdul-Jabbar has also worked as an actor, appearing in films such as Airplane! and Game of Death.

He is also a writer, with several books to his name including a best-selling memoir, Giant Steps.

Abdul-Jabbar has been active in social and political causes throughout his career, including civil rights and education reform.

He has received numerous awards and honors, including the Presidential Medal of Freedom from President Barack Obama in 2016.

DID YOU KNOW?

WHO AM I?

Name..

Nickname..

ABOUT ME

Skill

_____

Born

_____

Year Started

_____

INTERESTING FACTS ABOUT ME

1 _____

2 _____

3 _____

Kareem Abdul-Jabbar was a talented and dedicated football player who inspired countless children with his skill and determination on the field. He was born on April 16, 1947 in New York City, and grew up in a rough neighborhood where he learned the value of hard work and perseverance from a young age.

Despite facing many challenges and setbacks throughout his career, Kareem remained determined to succeed and achieve his goals. He worked tirelessly to improve his skills and become one of the best football players in the world, and his dedication and determination paid off in the end.

As a child, Kareem had always been passionate about sports, especially football. He spent countless hours practicing and perfecting his skills on the field, and he quickly became known as one of the best players in his school and community.

Despite his talent and dedication, Kareem faced many obstacles and setbacks along the way. He often struggled with racism and discrimination, and he had to overcome many challenges in order to succeed.

Despite these challenges, Kareem refused to let them get in the way of his dreams. He remained focused and determined, and he worked harder than ever to achieve his goals.

As he grew older, Kareem's hard work and dedication paid off. He was eventually recruited by some of the best football teams in the country, and he became one of the most respected and successful players in the league.

Throughout his career, Kareem inspired countless children with his skill and determination on the field. He showed them that with hard work and perseverance, anything is possible.

Kareem's story is one of hope and inspiration, and it is a powerful reminder to all children that they can achieve their dreams no matter what obstacles they may face.

So if you are a child reading this story, take inspiration from Kareem's journey and remember that with hard work and determination, you can achieve anything you set your mind to. Don't let anyone or anything hold you back from reaching your goals and making your dreams a reality.

With a little hard work and determination, you too can achieve greatness just like Kareem Abdul-Jabbar. So never give up and always believe in yourself, because with hard work and perseverance, anything is possible.

Tim Duncan

Tim Duncan was born on April 25, 1976, in Christiansted, Virgin Islands.

He played college basketball at Wake Forest University, where he was a two-time National Player of the Year.

Duncan was the first overall pick in the 1997 NBA Draft by the San Antonio Spurs.

He played his entire career with the Spurs, winning five NBA championships (1999, 2003, 2005, 2007, 2014).

Duncan is a 15-time NBA All-Star and a 15-time All-NBA selection.

He was named NBA Finals MVP three times (1999, 2003, 2005) and the NBA's Regular Season MVP twice (2002, 2003).

Duncan is known for his fundamental and unselfish style of play, earning him the nickname "The Big Fundamental."

He is widely considered one of the greatest power forwards in NBA history.

Duncan is a philanthropist and has been involved in various charitable efforts throughout his career, including founding the Tim Duncan Foundation to raise money for children and families in need.

Duncan retired from the NBA in 2016 and was inducted into the Basketball Hall of Fame in 2020.

DID YOU KNOW?

WHO AM I?

Name..

Nickname..

ABOUT ME

Skill

_____

Born

_____

Year Started

_____

INTERESTING FACTS ABOUT ME

1 _____

2 _____

3 _____

Tim Duncan was a young boy who loved playing football. He loved the feeling of the ball in his hands, the thrill of scoring a goal, and the camaraderie he felt with his teammates. Tim was always the first one to arrive at practice and the last one to leave, determined to become the best football player he could be.

As he grew older, Tim's talent for the game became more and more apparent. He was fast, agile, and had an incredible ability to anticipate the movements of his opponents. His coaches and teammates were amazed by his skills and determination, and they knew that he had a bright future ahead of him.

Despite his talent, Tim never let it go to his head. He remained humble and worked tirelessly to improve his game. He spent hours practicing his ball handling, his shooting, and his passing, determined to become the best he could be.

As Tim's skills continued to improve, he began to attract the attention of top football clubs around the world. He was offered contracts and lucrative deals, but Tim knew that his true passion was for the game itself, not the fame and fortune that came with it.

So, he chose to sign with a smaller club that was passionate about the game and had a strong sense of community. Tim knew that this was where he could truly thrive as a player and make a real difference in the world.

And thrive he did. Tim quickly became one of the top players in the league, leading his team to numerous championships and accolades. He was a natural leader on and off the field, always putting his team and their success above his own.

Despite his success, Tim remained humble and focused on his game. He never let the fame and attention go to his head, always staying true to himself and his love for football.

As Tim's career began to wind down, he knew that it was time to pass the torch to the next generation of talented young football players. He spent his final years mentoring and coaching young players, sharing his love and knowledge of the game with them.

Tim's legacy as a football player will live on forever, inspiring generations of young players to pursue their dreams and work hard to achieve their goals. His dedication, determination, and humility serve as a shining example of what it means to be a true athlete and a role model.

Oscar Robertson

Oscar Robertson, also known as "The Big O," was a professional basketball player who played for the Cincinnati Royals and the Milwaukee Bucks.

Robertson was a versatile player who could play multiple positions, including point guard and shooting guard.

He was a 12-time NBA All-Star and a member of the 1971-1972 Milwaukee Bucks team that won the NBA championship.

Robertson was the first player in NBA history to average a triple-double (double digits in three statistical categories) for an entire season. He achieved this feat in the 1961-1962 season and repeated it in the 1962-1963 season.

Robertson was also the first player in NBA history to record a triple-double in the NBA Finals. He accomplished this in 1971 against the Baltimore Bullets.

Robertson was known for his excellent ball-handling skills and court vision, which allowed him to rack up assists and lead his team to victory.

He was inducted into the Naismith Memorial Basketball Hall of Fame in 1980.

Robertson was born on November 24, 1938 in Charlotte, Tennessee.

In addition to his success on the court, Robertson was also an accomplished businessman and philanthropist.

After retiring from basketball, Robertson became an advocate for the rights of NBA players and played a key role in the formation of the National Basketball Players Association (NBPA). He served as the union's president from 1964 to 1974 and was instrumental in securing better wages and working conditions for NBA players.

DID YOU KNOW?

WHO AM I?

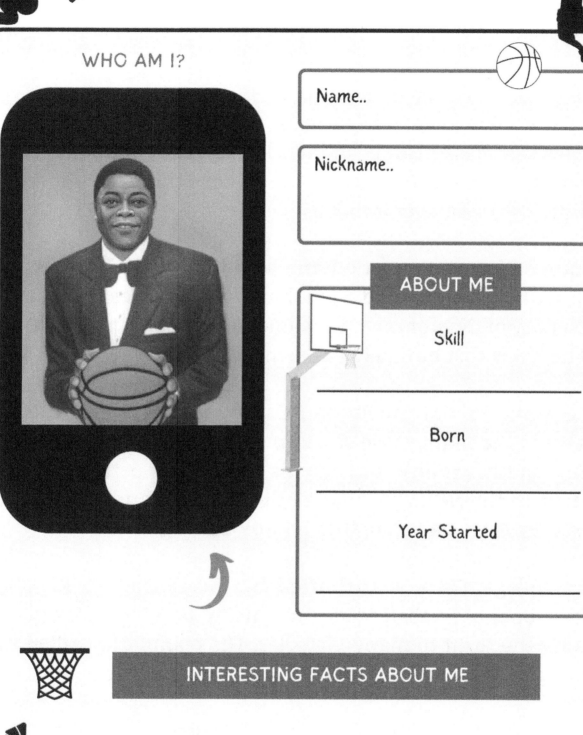

Name..

Nickname..

ABOUT ME

Skill

_____

Born

_____

Year Started

_____

INTERESTING FACTS ABOUT ME

1 _____

2 _____

3 _____

There was once a young boy named Oscar Robertson who lived in a small town in Indiana. Oscar had always been passionate about basketball and spent hours practicing every day. His hard work and dedication paid off, as he quickly became one of the best players on his school's team.

As Oscar got older, he began to dream of becoming a professional basketball player. He knew that it would take a lot of hard work and determination to achieve this goal, but he was willing to do whatever it took.

Oscar continued to work hard and improve his skills, and eventually he was offered a scholarship to play basketball at the University of Cincinnati. This was a huge opportunity for Oscar, and he knew that he had to make the most of it.

During his time at Cincinnati, Oscar became one of the best players in the country. He was known for his impressive scoring ability and his ability to make his teammates better. His team made it to the NCAA tournament every year, and in his senior year, they even made it to the championship game.

After college, Oscar was drafted by the Cincinnati Royals, a professional basketball team. He quickly became a star player, leading the team to many victories. His teammates called him "The Big O," because he was such a dominant player.

Oscar's career was full of accomplishments and accolades. He was named the NBA Most Valuable Player award three times, and he was selected to the All-NBA First Team ten times.

He was also a member of the United States Olympic basketball team that won the gold medal in the 1964 games.

Despite all of his success, Oscar never let it go to his head. He always stayed humble and gracious, and he worked hard to be a good role model for young basketball players.

Oscar's impact on the game of basketball was immense, and he is considered one of the greatest players of all time. He inspired countless young people to pursue their dreams, and his legacy lives on today.

So if you're a young basketball player with big dreams, just remember the story of Oscar Robertson. With hard work, dedication, and a never-give-up attitude, you too can achieve greatness.

Hakeem Olajuwon

Hakeem Olajuwon was born in Lagos, Nigeria on January 21, 1963.

He was originally a soccer player before switching to basketball at the age of 15.

Olajuwon was a two-time NCAA champion while attending the University of Houston.

He was the first overall pick in the 1984 NBA Draft, selected by the Houston Rockets.

Olajuwon won two NBA championships with the Rockets in 1994 and 1995.

He was a 12-time NBA All-Star and was named to the All-NBA First Team five times.

Olajuwon was named the NBA Defensive Player of the Year twice, in 1993 and 1994.

He holds the record for most blocked shots in a single season with 318 in the 1990-1991 season.

Olajuwon is the only player in NBA history to win the NBA MVP, NBA Finals MVP, and NBA Defensive Player of the Year awards in the same season (1994).

After retiring from the NBA in 2002, Olajuwon converted to Islam and changed his name to Hakeem Abdul Olajuwon.

DID YOU KNOW?

WHO AM I?

Name..

Nickname..

ABOUT ME

Skill

_____

Born

_____

Year Started

_____

INTERESTING FACTS ABOUT ME

 1 _____

 2 _____

 3 _____

Hakeem Olajuwon was a basketball player who had a dream of becoming a professional athlete. He was born in Lagos, Nigeria and grew up playing soccer and basketball. Hakeem was tall and had a natural talent for sports, but he knew that he had to work hard to achieve his dream.

As a child, Hakeem spent hours practicing his basketball skills. He would shoot hoops in his backyard, run laps around the neighborhood, and train with his older brother, who was also a talented athlete. Hakeem was determined to become the best basketball player he could be.

Despite his dedication to the sport, Hakeem faced many challenges. He was often teased and bullied by his classmates because of his height and love of basketball. But Hakeem refused to let these negative experiences discourage him. He knew that he had a passion for the game, and he was determined to succeed.

One day, Hakeem's hard work and dedication paid off. He was offered a scholarship to play basketball at the University of Houston. This was a huge opportunity for Hakeem, and he knew that he had to seize it. He worked even harder in college, practicing every day and perfecting his skills.

Hakeem's talent and dedication did not go unnoticed. He was noticed by professional scouts, and in 1984, he was drafted by the Houston Rockets in the NBA. Hakeem was thrilled to be given this opportunity and worked even harder to become a star player.

Over the years, Hakeem proved to be a fierce competitor on the court. He was known for his quick reflexes, strong defense, and impressive scoring ability. He was also a leader and role model for his teammates, always encouraging and supporting them.

Hakeem's hard work and determination paid off, and he became one of the greatest basketball players of all time. He won two NBA championships with the Rockets, was named an All-Star numerous times, and was inducted into the Basketball Hall of Fame.

But Hakeem's accomplishments went beyond just his sports achievements. He was also a philanthropist and mentor to many young athletes. He founded the Hakeem Olajuwon Foundation, which provided resources and opportunities for underprivileged children to participate in sports and other activities.

Hakeem's story is one of determination, hard work, and perseverance. He never let his challenges or setbacks hold him back, and he always believed in himself and his dreams. He is a true inspiration to children and adults alike, and his legacy will continue to inspire generations to come.

Jerry West

Jerry West was born on May 28, 1938 in Chelyan, West Virginia.

He played college basketball at West Virginia University, where he was a two-time consensus All-American.

West was drafted by the Minneapolis Lakers in the 1960 NBA Draft, and played with the team until they moved to Los Angeles in 1960.

He was a 14-time NBA All-Star, and was named to the All-NBA First Team 10 times.

West won an NBA championship with the Lakers in 1972, and was named the Finals MVP.

He was also a member of the United States men's Olympic basketball team, which won a gold medal in Rome in 1960.

West retired from playing in 1974, and went on to serve as a coach and executive for several NBA teams, including the Lakers and the Golden State Warriors.

He is often referred to as "Mr. Clutch," due to his ability to perform in pressure situations and hit game-winning shots.

West was inducted into the Naismith Memorial Basketball Hall of Fame in 1979.

In 1996, West was named one of the 50 Greatest Players in NBA History.

DID YOU KNOW?

WHO AM I?

Name..

Nickname..

ABOUT ME

Skill

_____

Born

_____

Year Started

_____

INTERESTING FACTS ABOUT ME

 1 _____

 2 _____

 3 _____

Jerry West was a basketball player who was known for his determination and hard work. He was a role model for many young basketball players, and his story is one that is sure to inspire and motivate children of all ages.

West was born in Chelyan, West Virginia in 1938. He was the youngest of six children, and his parents were poor coal miners. Despite their financial struggles, West's parents always encouraged him to follow his dreams and to work hard.

West began playing basketball at a young age, and he quickly became known for his incredible talent and dedication. He practiced for hours each day, working tirelessly to improve his skills. His hard work paid off, and he was eventually offered a scholarship to play basketball at West Virginia University.

At West Virginia, West excelled on the court and quickly became one of the best players in the country. He led his team to the NCAA Championship in 1959, and he was named the tournament's Most Outstanding Player. After graduating from college, West was drafted by the Los Angeles Lakers, where he would spend the majority of his professional career.

West was an incredible basketball player, and he was known for his fierce competitive spirit and his ability to always give 100% on the court. He was a leader on the Lakers team, and he helped lead the team to numerous victories throughout his career.

Despite his many accomplishments, West faced his fair share of challenges and setbacks.

He suffered numerous injuries throughout his career, and he often had to work hard to overcome them. But he never let these setbacks discourage him, and he always stayed focused on his goals.

West's determination and hard work paid off, and he was eventually inducted into the Basketball Hall of Fame. He was also named one of the 50 Greatest Players in NBA History.

Despite his many accomplishments, West never let fame and success go to his head. He was always humble and gracious, and he used his platform to give back to his community. He was known for his charitable work, and he often worked with children to help inspire and motivate them to pursue their own dreams.

West's story is one of perseverance and hard work, and it is sure to inspire children of all ages. His determination and dedication are a testament to the fact that with hard work and determination, anyone can achieve their goals.

Children can learn so much from Jerry West's story. They can learn that no matter what challenges and setbacks they may face, they can overcome them with hard work and determination. They can also learn that it is important to stay humble and gracious, even when they achieve success.

Jerry West's story is a reminder to all children that with hard work and determination, they can achieve anything they set their minds to. So let his story be a source of inspiration and motivation for children everywhere, and let them know that they can accomplish anything they put their hearts and minds to.

Julius Erving

Julius Erving, also known as "Dr. J." was born in Hempstead, New York in 1950.

He attended Roosevelt High School in Long Island, where he excelled in basketball and track and field.

Erving played college basketball at the University of Massachusetts, where he averaged 26.3 points and 20.2 rebounds per game.

He was drafted by the American Basketball Association's Virginia Squires in 1971, and went on to become one of the league's biggest stars.

Erving was known for his high-flying acrobatics and electrifying dunks, which helped popularize the ABA and eventually the NBA.

In 1976, Erving joined the NBA's Philadelphia 76ers and led the team to the NBA Championship in 1983.

He was named the NBA's Most Valuable Player in 1981 and was a 11-time NBA All-Star.

Erving was inducted into the Naismith Memorial Basketball Hall of Fame in 1993.

After his playing career, Erving became a successful businessman and philanthropist, founding a number of companies and charities.

In addition to his basketball career, Erving was also a skilled golfer and skier, and often participated in charity golf tournaments and ski events.

DID YOU KNOW?

WHO AM I?

Name..

Nickname..

ABOUT ME

Skill

_____

Born

_____

Year Started

_____

INTERESTING FACTS ABOUT ME

1 _____

2 _____

3 _____

There was once a young boy named Julius Erving, who lived in a small town in New York. From the moment he was born, Julius had a passion for basketball. He would spend hours in the backyard practicing his jump shot, dribbling through cones, and working on his footwork.

As he grew older, Julius's love for the game only grew stronger. He would spend every free moment he had on the basketball court, whether it was at the local park or in the school gym. His friends and family knew that Julius was destined for greatness on the court, and they encouraged him to pursue his dreams.

Despite the challenges he faced, Julius never gave up on his love for basketball. He spent countless hours training, practicing, and honing his skills. He knew that if he worked hard enough, he could achieve his dream of becoming a professional basketball player.

As Julius entered high school, he began to stand out as a talented athlete. He led his team to the state championship and was named the most valuable player. His skills and determination caught the attention of college coaches, and Julius was offered scholarships to play at some of the top basketball programs in the country.

Julius chose to attend the University of Massachusetts, where he continued to excel on the court. He led the team to the NCAA tournament and was named an All-American. After just two years of college, Julius decided to enter the NBA draft.

In 1971, Julius was selected by the Virginia Squires in the American Basketball Association (ABA) draft. He quickly became a star in the league, leading the Squires to the championship in his first season. Julius's impressive performance on the court earned him the nickname "Dr. J," and he became one of the most exciting players in the game.

In 1976, Julius joined the Philadelphia 76ers in the NBA. He continued to shine on the court, leading the team to the championship in 1983. Julius was named the MVP of the Finals and was inducted into the Basketball Hall of Fame in 1993.

Throughout his career, Julius inspired countless young people to pursue their dreams and never give up. He proved that with hard work and dedication, anything is possible. Julius's legacy lives on today as a symbol of what can be achieved through perseverance and determination.

For young children who dream of becoming basketball players, Julius's story is a source of inspiration. It shows them that no matter where they come from or what challenges they face, they can achieve greatness if they work hard and never give up.

Julius's life is a testament to the power of hard work and determination. He never let obstacles stand in his way, and he never stopped believing in himself. Through his dedication and determination, Julius became one of the greatest basketball players of all time.

For young children who dream of achieving their own goals, Julius's story is a reminder that anything is possible if they are willing to put in the hard work and never give up. His legacy serves as an inspiration to all who seek to achieve their dreams and make a positive impact on the world.

John Havlicek

John Havlicek was born on April 8, 1940 in Martins Ferry, Ohio.

He played college basketball at Ohio State University, where he was a two-time All-American and led the Buckeyes to the 1960 NCAA Championship.

Havlicek was selected by the Boston Celtics with the seventh overall pick in the 1962 NBA Draft.

During his 16-year career with the Celtics, Havlicek won eight NBA championships and was named to the All-NBA First Team four times.

Havlicek was known for his tireless work ethic and was one of the most durable players in NBA history, appearing in 1,270 games and missing just 22 games due to injury.

He was a 13-time NBA All-Star and was inducted into the Naismith Memorial Basketball Hall of Fame in 1984.

Havlicek was also a member of the 1972 U.S. Olympic team, which won a gold medal in Munich.

He was the leading scorer in Celtics history when he retired in 1978, a record that stood until it was broken by Larry Bird in 1992.

Havlicek's number 17 jersey was retired by the Celtics in 1978, and he was named one of the 50 greatest players in NBA history in 1996.

After retiring from basketball, Havlicek owned and operated a successful real estate business in Ohio. He passed away on April 25, 2019 at the age of 79.

DID YOU KNOW?

WHO AM I?

Name..

Nickname..

ABOUT ME

Skill
_____

Born
_____

Year Started
_____

INTERESTING FACTS ABOUT ME

 1 _____

 2 _____

 3 _____

John Havlicek was a legendary basketball player who spent his entire career with the Boston Celtics. Known for his relentless energy and competitive spirit, Havlicek was a key player in the team's eight championship victories during the 1960s and 1970s.

Havlicek grew up in Ohio, where he played basketball in high school and college. Despite his natural talent for the game, he faced many challenges and setbacks along the way. But he never let those obstacles hold him back. Instead, Havlicek used them as motivation to work harder and become the best player he could be.

One of Havlicek's most memorable moments came in the 1965 Eastern Conference Finals, when he hit a game-winning shot in overtime against the Philadelphia 76ers. The shot, which became known as "The Steal," helped the Celtics advance to the NBA Finals and eventually win the championship.

But Havlicek's impact on the game went far beyond just one shot. He was known for his consistent performance, playing in 1,270 games and scoring over 26,000 points in his career. He was also a strong defensive player, earning eight All-Defensive Team selections and being named to the NBA's 50th Anniversary All-Time Team.

Despite all of his achievements on the court, Havlicek was also a role model off of it. He was known for his sportsmanship and humility, always giving credit to his teammates and coaches for his successes.

Havlicek's dedication to hard work and teamwork served as an inspiration to countless young basketball players. He showed them that with determination and perseverance, they could achieve their dreams, no matter how difficult they may seem.

One young basketball player who was particularly inspired by Havlicek was a boy named Timmy. Timmy was a talented athlete, but he often struggled with self-doubt and a tendency to give up when things got tough.

One day, Timmy's coach showed the team a video of Havlicek's famous "The Steal" shot. As Timmy watched Havlicek's relentless pursuit of the ball and his refusal to give up, he was struck by the player's determination and drive.

Timmy began to see that, just like Havlicek, he had the ability to overcome any obstacle and succeed if he put in the hard work and effort. He started to believe in himself and his teammates, and his performance on the court improved dramatically.

As the season went on, Timmy's confidence grew and he began to take on a leadership role on his team. He encouraged his teammates to never give up and to always strive to be their best.

Thanks to Havlicek's example, Timmy learned that anything was possible if he stayed committed and worked hard. He went on to become one of the top players on his high school team, and even earned a scholarship to play college basketball.

Timmy's story is just one example of the many children who were inspired by John Havlicek's dedication to excellence and hard work. Havlicek's legacy will continue to inspire young athletes for generations to come, reminding them that with hard work and determination, they can achieve their dreams and make a positive impact in the world.

Bob Cousy

Bob Cousy played basketball for the Boston Celtics from 1950 to 1963.

He was known for his flashy ball-handling skills and innovative playmaking abilities.

Cousy was a 13-time NBA All-Star and was named the league's Most Valuable Player in 1957.

He was also a member of the 1952 U.S. Olympic basketball team, which won a gold medal in Helsinki.

Cousy's nickname was "Houdini of the Hardwood" due to his ability to escape tight defensive situations with his ball-handling skills.

He was inducted into the Naismith Memorial Basketball Hall of Fame in 1971.

Cousy was also an accomplished coach, leading Boston College to the NCAA tournament in his first year as head coach in 1973.

He was the first player to win the NBA's assists title in the 1952-53 season, and he led the league in assists for eight straight seasons from 1953 to 1960.

Cousy was known for his sportsmanship and was named to the NBA's 50th Anniversary All-Time Team in 1996.

He also had a successful career as a television commentator and served as the head coach of the Cincinnati Royals from 1969 to 1973.

DID YOU KNOW?

WHO AM I?

Name..

Nickname..

ABOUT ME

Skill

_____

Born

_____

Year Started

_____

INTERESTING FACTS ABOUT ME

1. _____
2. _____
3. _____

Bob Cousy was a basketball player who was born in the year 1928. He grew up in a small town in New York, and from a young age, he showed a natural talent for basketball. As he grew older, he began to play for his high school team and quickly became one of the best players in the league.

When he graduated from high school, Cousy was recruited by several top universities to play basketball for their teams. He ultimately decided to attend Holy Cross College, where he played for their team, the Crusaders.

Cousy quickly made a name for himself at Holy Cross, leading the team to numerous victories and earning a reputation as one of the best players in the country. He was a master at passing the ball and was known for his quick reflexes and agility on the court.

After he graduated from Holy Cross, Cousy was drafted by the Boston Celtics, a professional basketball team. He joined the team in the 1950s and quickly became one of their star players. He led the team to several championships and was named the Most Valuable Player of the NBA in the 1957 season.

Throughout his career, Cousy was known for his sportsmanship and humility. He always put the team first and worked hard to improve his own skills and help his teammates succeed. He was a role model for young basketball players and inspired many children to pursue their dreams.

One of Cousy's most memorable moments came in the 1957 championship game against the St. Louis Hawks. The game was tied with only seconds left on the clock, and the ball was in Cousy's hands. He faked a shot, then passed the ball to his teammate Bill Russell, who made the game-winning basket.

The crowd went wild, and Cousy was hailed as a hero. But he refused to take all the credit, saying that it was a team effort and that he was just glad to have been able to contribute.

After retiring from basketball, Cousy remained active in the sport, coaching and mentoring young players. He also became involved in various charitable causes and was known for his generosity and kindness.

Cousy's legacy lives on to this day, and he is remembered as one of the greatest basketball players of all time. His determination, hard work, and sportsmanship are an inspiration to children everywhere, and he serves as a reminder that with dedication and perseverance, anyone can achieve their dreams.

Kevin Garnett

Kevin Garnett was drafted out of high school in 1995, becoming the first player in 20 years to do so.

He played for the Minnesota Timberwolves for 12 seasons before being traded to the Boston Celtics in 2007.

Garnett is a 15-time NBA All-Star and has won an MVP award and a championship with the Celtics in 2008.

He is known for his intense passion and intensity on the court, earning him the nickname "The Big Ticket."

Garnett has a philanthropic side, establishing the Kevin Garnett Family Life Center in his hometown of Mauldin, South Carolina to provide resources for young people.

He has a close friendship with former teammate Paul Pierce, with the two often referred to as "The Truth" and "The Big Ticket."

Garnett has a love for fashion and has even started his own clothing line, "Area 21."

He is a devout Christian and has credited his faith for helping him through difficult times in his career.

Garnett has a deep respect for the history of the game, often seeking out advice from former players and coaches.

Despite his tough reputation on the court, Garnett is known to be a kind and generous person off the court, often donating to charities and supporting various causes.

DID YOU KNOW?

WHO AM I?

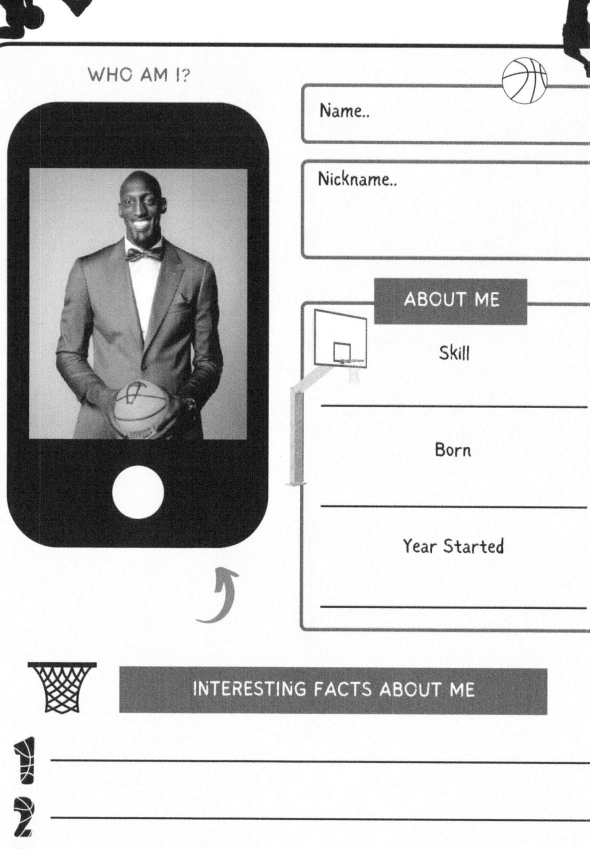

Name..

Nickname..

ABOUT ME

Skill

_____

Born

_____

Year Started

_____

INTERESTING FACTS ABOUT ME

1 _____

2 _____

3 _____

There was once a young boy named Kevin Garnett who had a dream of becoming a professional basketball player. Despite being told that he was too small and not good enough to make it in the world of sports, Kevin refused to give up on his dream.

As a child, Kevin was always fascinated by the game of basketball. He would spend hours practicing his jump shot, learning new moves, and working on his ball handling skills. He knew that if he worked hard enough, he could become one of the best players in the world.

As Kevin grew older, he began to play for his high school basketball team. He quickly became one of the best players on the team, and his coaches knew that he had a bright future ahead of him.

Despite his success on the court, Kevin still faced many challenges and setbacks. He was often underestimated by his opponents, and many people doubted his ability to succeed at the highest level.

But Kevin never let these obstacles get in his way. He continued to work hard and strive for excellence, and eventually, he was offered a scholarship to play college basketball at the University of Minnesota.

During his time at Minnesota, Kevin became one of the best players in the country. He was a dominant force on the court, and his leadership and determination inspired his teammates to give their all every game.

In 1995, Kevin decided to enter the NBA draft, and he was selected as the fifth overall pick by the Minnesota Timberwolves. It was a dream come true for Kevin, and he knew that it was just the beginning of his journey to greatness.

Over the next few years, Kevin worked tirelessly to improve his game and become a leader on the court. He was named an All-Star for the first time in 1997, and he quickly became one of the most respected and feared players in the league.

As Kevin's career continued to rise, he faced many more challenges and setbacks. He faced criticism from the media and opponents who doubted his ability to lead a team to a championship. But Kevin never let these obstacles get in his way. He continued to work hard, lead by example, and never give up on his dream.

In 2008, Kevin's hard work and dedication finally paid off. He was traded to the Boston Celtics, and he helped lead the team to an NBA championship that year. It was a moment that Kevin had dreamed of since he was a child, and it was a testament to his unwavering determination and resilience.

Today, Kevin Garnett is considered one of the greatest basketball players of all time. He is a role model for aspiring athletes all over the world, and his story serves as an inspiration to never give up on your dreams no matter how difficult they may seem.

So if you are a young athlete with a dream, take a page out of Kevin Garnett's book and never give up. With hard work, determination, and a little bit of luck, you too can achieve greatness and make your dreams a reality.

Elgin Baylor

Elgin Baylor was born on September 16, 1934 in Washington, D.C.

He played college basketball at Seattle University and led the team to the NCAA Division I Championship in 1958.

He was drafted by the Minneapolis Lakers in the first round of the NBA draft in 1958 and played for the team until 1971.

Baylor was a dominant force in the NBA and was a 10-time All-Star and 11-time All-NBA selection.

He led the Lakers to eight NBA Finals appearances and was a member of the 1972 championship team.

Baylor was known for his impressive scoring ability and was the first player in NBA history to score more than 70 points in a single game.

He was also a skilled passer and rebounder and led the league in scoring and rebounds in different seasons.

In 1977, Baylor was inducted into the Basketball Hall of Fame.

After retiring from playing, Baylor became a coach and served as head coach of the New Orleans Jazz and the Los Angeles Clippers.

He was also a successful businessman and owned a real estate company in the Los Angeles area.

DID YOU KNOW?

WHO AM I?

Name..

Nickname..

ABOUT ME

Skill

_____

Born

_____

Year Started

_____

INTERESTING FACTS ABOUT ME

 1 _____

 2 _____

 3 _____

Elgin Baylor was a man who dedicated his life to basketball and became one of the greatest players in history. He was a man of great skill, determination, and perseverance, and his story is one that can inspire children to pursue their passions and never give up on their dreams.

Elgin Baylor was born in Washington D.C. in 1934. From a young age, he was passionate about basketball and spent hours practicing and perfecting his game. Despite his small stature, he had an incredible talent for the sport and was always eager to learn and improve.

As he grew older, Elgin began to receive recognition for his skills on the court. He attended Spingarn High School in D.C. and was a star player on the school's varsity team. In his senior year, he led the team to the city championship and was named the Most Valuable Player of the tournament.

After high school, Elgin received a scholarship to play basketball at Seattle University. There, he continued to excel on the court and was named an All-American in his junior and senior years. He was also a key member of the team that won the NCAA Championship in 1958.

After college, Elgin was drafted by the Minneapolis Lakers of the NBA. He quickly became one of the league's top players, leading the Lakers to eight NBA Finals appearances and one championship in 1972. He was a ten-time All-Star and was inducted into the Basketball Hall of Fame in 1977.

But Elgin's journey to greatness was not always easy. He faced many challenges and setbacks along the way, but he never let them hold him back. He worked hard every day to improve his skills and overcome his weaknesses, and he never stopped believing in himself.

One of the biggest challenges Elgin faced was racism. During his time in the NBA, black players were often treated unfairly and subjected to discrimination. Elgin experienced this firsthand and fought against it throughout his career. He used his platform to speak out against racism and promote equality and justice.

Elgin's determination and perseverance were also evident off the court. In 1971, he suffered a serious knee injury that forced him to retire from the Lakers. But instead of letting this setback defeat him, he used it as an opportunity to pursue other passions. He became a coach and eventually a general manager for the Los Angeles Clippers, helping to build the team into a contender.

Elgin's story is one of inspiration and determination. He proved that with hard work and perseverance, anyone can achieve their dreams, no matter how difficult the journey may be. He is a role model for children everywhere, and his legacy will always be remembered as one of the greatest basketball players of all time.

Scottie Pippen

Scottie Pippen was born on September 25, 1965 in Hamburg, Arkansas.

Pippen was a standout high school basketball player and played college basketball at the University of Central Arkansas.

Pippen was selected by the Seattle SuperSonics with the fifth overall pick in the 1987 NBA Draft, but was traded to the Chicago Bulls on draft day.

Pippen played small forward for the Bulls and was a member of the "Bulls Dynasty" that won six NBA championships in the 1990s.

Pippen was known for his defensive skills and was named to the NBA All-Defensive Team eight times.

Pippen was also a seven-time NBA All-Star and was inducted into the Naismith Memorial Basketball Hall of Fame in 2010.

Pippen played for the Bulls from 1987-1998, and then played for the Houston Rockets, Portland Trail Blazers, and the Bulls again before retiring in 2004.

Pippen's number 33 jersey was retired by the Chicago Bulls in 2005.

Pippen is the only NBA player to have won an NBA championship and an Olympic gold medal in the same year, which he achieved in 1992 and 1996.

Pippen's younger brother, Brent, also played college basketball at the University of Central Arkansas.

DID YOU KNOW?

WHO AM I?

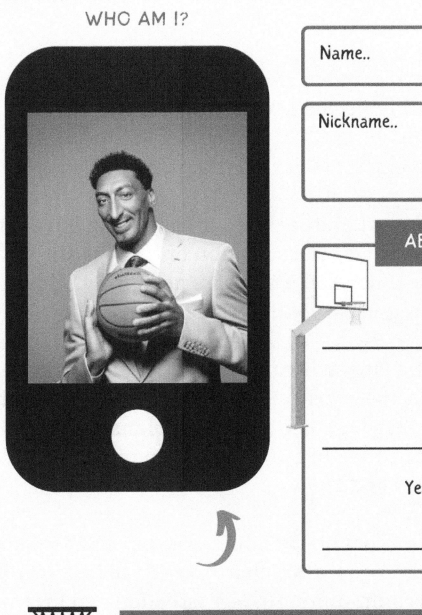

Name..

Nickname..

ABOUT ME

Skill

_____

Born

_____

Year Started

_____

INTERESTING FACTS ABOUT ME

 1 _____

 2 _____

 3 _____

Scottie Pippen was always a natural athlete. From the time he was a young boy, he loved playing basketball and dreamed of one day becoming a professional player. He practiced every day, honing his skills and working hard to become the best basketball player he could be.

As he grew older, Scottie's talent and dedication paid off. He was a star player on his high school team, leading them to many victories and earning himself a scholarship to play college basketball at the University of Central Arkansas.

Scottie continued to excel on the court at college, and his hard work and talent soon caught the attention of the NBA. In 1987, he was drafted to the Chicago Bulls, where he quickly became a star player and an integral part of the team's success.

Over the years, Scottie Pippen became known as one of the best basketball players in the world. He was a key player on the Chicago Bulls team that won six NBA championships, and he was also a member of the United States Olympic gold medal winning teams in 1992 and 1996.

But Scottie Pippen's success on the court was just one aspect of his life. He was also known for his charity work and dedication to giving back to his community. He regularly donated his time and resources to help underprivileged children and families, and he worked to raise awareness about important social issues.

For young children dreaming of one day becoming a great basketball player, Scottie Pippen's story is an inspiration.

His hard work and dedication to the sport, combined with his commitment to giving back to his community, make him a role model for all children to look up to.

But Scottie's story is also a reminder that success doesn't come easy. It takes hard work, determination, and a willingness to never give up on your dreams. As Scottie himself said, "You have to have the mindset that you're going to be the best, and you have to work towards it every day."

So for all the young children out there dreaming of one day becoming a great basketball player, remember Scottie Pippen's story. Believe in yourself, work hard, and never give up on your dreams. With hard work and dedication, anything is possible.

Charles Barkley

Charles Barkley was born on February 20, 1963 in Leeds, Alabama.

He played college basketball at Auburn University before being drafted by the Philadelphia 76ers in 1984.

Barkley was a 11-time NBA All-Star and was named to the All-NBA First Team five times.

He won an Olympic gold medal in 1992 as a member of the United States Men's Olympic Basketball Team, known as the "Dream Team."

Barkley was inducted into the Naismith Memorial Basketball Hall of Fame in 2006.

He has worked as an NBA analyst for TNT's Inside the NBA since 2000.

Barkley is known for his outspoken personality and has made controversial comments on various social and political issues.

He has also been involved in several legal issues, including a DUI arrest and a gambling debt.

In addition to his basketball career, Barkley has also dabbled in acting and has made appearances in TV shows and movies such as Space Jam and The Simpsons.

Barkley is known for his charitable work and has raised millions of dollars for various causes through his Charles Barkley Foundation.

Charles Barkley

DID YOU KNOW?

WHO AM I?

Name..

Nickname..

ABOUT ME

Skill

_____

Born

_____

Year Started

_____

INTERESTING FACTS ABOUT ME

 1 _____

 2 _____

 3 _____

Charles Barkley was a basketball player who inspired many children to follow their dreams. He was known for his big personality and his amazing skills on the court.

Born in 1963 in Leeds, Alabama, Charles had a passion for basketball from a young age. He played for his high school team and quickly became a star player. After high school, he attended Auburn University where he played for the Tigers. He was known for his strong rebounding abilities and his ability to score points.

After college, Charles was drafted by the Philadelphia 76ers in 1984. He quickly made a name for himself as a dominant player in the league. He was named an All-Star in his first season and continued to be a star player for the 76ers for many years.

In 1992, Charles joined the Phoenix Suns and became one of the team's leaders. He led the Suns to the NBA Finals in 1993, where they lost to the Chicago Bulls. Despite the loss, Charles was praised for his outstanding performance in the playoffs.

In 1996, Charles joined the Houston Rockets and helped lead the team to the NBA Championship in his first season with the team. He retired from the NBA in 2000 with many accolades and awards, including being named one of the 50 greatest players in NBA history.

Throughout his career, Charles inspired children to pursue their dreams and work hard to achieve them. He was known for his strong work ethic and dedication to the game.

He always encouraged young players to practice hard and never give up, no matter how difficult things may seem.

One young boy who was inspired by Charles was Marcus, a seventh-grade basketball player. Marcus had always dreamed of playing in the NBA one day, just like Charles. He practiced every day and worked hard to improve his skills.

One day, Marcus received the opportunity of a lifetime. He was invited to a basketball camp led by Charles Barkley himself. Marcus was overjoyed and couldn't wait to meet his hero and learn from him.

At the camp, Charles spent hours working with the young players, teaching them new skills and techniques. He encouraged them to always believe in themselves and never give up. Marcus was in awe of Charles's talent and dedication to the game.

After the camp, Marcus returned home with a renewed sense of determination. He practiced harder than ever before and worked on improving his skills. His coach noticed his improvement and began to play him more in games.

As the season went on, Marcus's confidence grew and he became one of the best players on his team. He led his team to the championship game and scored the winning basket in the final seconds of the game.

After the game, Marcus was interviewed by the local news. He was asked about his hero, Charles Barkley, and how he inspired him. Marcus told the reporter about the basketball camp and how Charles had encouraged him to never give up and always believe in himself.

Thanks to Charles's inspiration and guidance, Marcus was able to achieve his dream of becoming a successful basketball player. He knew that he couldn't have done it without Charles's help and was forever grateful for the opportunity to learn from him.

Charles Barkley's impact on children went far beyond the basketball court. He was a role model for many young people and showed them that with hard work and determination, they could achieve their dreams. His legacy will continue to inspire children for years to come.

Dwyane Wade

Dwyane Wade was born on January 17, 1982 in Chicago, Illinois.

He attended Marquette University, where he played college basketball for the Golden Eagles.

Wade was selected by the Miami Heat as the fifth overall pick in the 2003 NBA Draft.

He is a three-time NBA champion, winning titles with the Heat in 2006, 2012, and 2013.

Wade is a 13-time NBA All-Star, and has been named to the All-NBA First Team twice in his career.

He has also won an Olympic gold medal as a member of Team USA in the 2008 Beijing Olympics.

In 2011, he was named one of Time magazine's 100 Most Influential People.

Wade has his own production company called ZZ Productions, which has produced a number of documentary films and television shows.

He has been involved in a number of philanthropic efforts, including founding the Wade's World Foundation to support education and health initiatives.

In 2016, he published a memoir called "Father First: How My Life Became Bigger Than Basketball."

DID YOU KNOW?

WHO AM I?

Name..

Nickname..

ABOUT ME

Skill

_____

Born

_____

Year Started

_____

INTERESTING FACTS ABOUT ME

 _____

 _____

 _____

Dwyane Wade was a young boy growing up in Chicago, Illinois. He was always passionate about basketball and spent every moment he could practicing and playing the game. Despite being small in stature, Dwyane had a heart and determination that was unmatched by anyone on the court.

One day, Dwyane's high school basketball coach noticed his talent and dedication to the game. He pulled Dwyane aside and told him that with hard work and perseverance, he could go far in the world of basketball. Dwyane took these words to heart and worked tirelessly to improve his skills.

As he got older, Dwyane's dreams of becoming a professional basketball player became a reality. He was drafted to the NBA and joined the Miami Heat, where he quickly made a name for himself as one of the best players in the league.

But Dwyane's journey to success was not easy. He faced many challenges and setbacks along the way, but he never gave up. He continued to work hard and never let anything stand in the way of his dreams.

One of Dwyane's biggest challenges came when he suffered a serious injury on the court. It was a tough time for him, but he refused to let it get him down. Instead, he used it as an opportunity to get stronger and come back even better than before.

Through sheer hard work and determination, Dwyane was able to overcome his injury and lead his team to victory in the NBA Championship.

It was a moment of pure joy and triumph for him, and it showed that no matter what obstacles come your way, with hard work and perseverance, you can overcome them and achieve your goals.

Dwyane's story is a true inspiration to children everywhere. It shows that no matter where you come from or what challenges you face, with hard work and determination, you can achieve anything you set your mind to.

As Dwyane's career continued to flourish, he became a role model to countless children around the world. He used his platform to give back to his community, starting a charity to help underprivileged children in Miami and around the country.

Through his charitable work and his dedication to the game of basketball, Dwyane became a true hero to children everywhere. He showed that with hard work and a positive attitude, anything is possible.

Dwyane's story is a true testament to the power of hard work and determination. No matter what obstacles come your way, if you stay true to your dreams and never give up, you can achieve anything you set your mind to. So if you're a young child with big dreams, take inspiration from Dwyane and never let anyone or anything stand in the way of your goals. With hard work and perseverance, you too can achieve greatness.

Karl Malone

Karl Malone was born on July 24. 1963 in Summerfield. Louisiana.

He played college basketball at Louisiana Tech University before being drafted by the Utah Jazz in 1985.

Malone is considered one of the greatest power forwards in NBA history and was a 14-time NBA All-Star.

He is the second-leading scorer in NBA history with 36.928 points. only behind Kareem Abdul-Jabbar.

Malone was a two-time NBA Most Valuable Player and won the award in 1997 and 1999.

He played for the Utah Jazz for 18 seasons and then played one season with the Los Angeles Lakers before retiring in 2004.

Malone is known for his physical style of play and his ability to score in the post.

He won gold medals with Team USA at the 1992 and 1996 Summer Olympics.

Malone was inducted into the Naismith Memorial Basketball Hall of Fame in 2010.

After his playing career. Malone has owned and operated a number of successful businesses. including car dealerships and restaurants.

DID YOU KNOW?

WHO AM I?

Name..

Nickname..

ABOUT ME

Skill

_____

Born

_____

Year Started

_____

INTERESTING FACTS ABOUT ME

 1 _____

 2 _____

 3 _____

Karl Malone was a basketball player who was known for his incredible strength and determination on the court. He was born on July 24th, 1963 in Summerfield, Louisiana and grew up in a small town with his parents and siblings. Despite facing many challenges and hardships in his childhood, Karl never let his circumstances hold him back. He always had a love for basketball and spent every moment he could practicing and perfecting his skills.

Karl's passion for the game paid off when he was recruited to play for the Louisiana Tech University basketball team. He excelled on the court and quickly became one of the top players in the country. In 1985, Karl was drafted by the Utah Jazz and began his professional career.

Throughout his time with the Jazz, Karl was known for his fierce competitiveness and unyielding work ethic. He worked tirelessly to improve his game and became one of the most dominant players in the league. In addition to his impressive scoring and rebounding abilities, Karl was also known for his leadership skills and his ability to inspire and motivate his teammates.

Despite facing numerous injuries and setbacks throughout his career, Karl never let his setbacks get the best of him. He remained determined and focused, always striving to be the best player he could be. His dedication and hard work paid off when he was named the NBA's Most Valuable Player in 1997 and 1999, and he helped lead the Jazz to the NBA Finals twice.

Karl's impact on the game of basketball was undeniable. He was a role model and an inspiration to young basketball players everywhere, and his legacy lives on through the countless players who have followed in his footsteps.

For children who may be struggling to find their own path or who may be facing challenges, Karl's story is a powerful reminder that with hard work and determination, anything is possible. No matter what obstacles may come your way, you have the strength and resilience to overcome them.

Karl's journey to greatness was not an easy one, but he never let that stop him from pursuing his dreams. He knew that with hard work and dedication, he could achieve anything he set his mind to.

So for all the young children out there who are looking for a little bit of inspiration, take a page from Karl Malone's book. Remember that with hard work and determination, you can accomplish anything you set your mind to. You have the power within you to overcome any obstacle and achieve your dreams.

So don't let anything hold you back. Believe in yourself and your abilities, and never give up on your dreams. With hard work and determination, you can achieve greatness just like Karl Malone did.

Rick Barry

Rick Barry was born on March 28, 1944 in Elizabeth, New Jersey.

He attended Roselle Park High School in Roselle Park, New Jersey, where he was a standout basketball player.

After high school, Barry attended the University of Miami, where he played college basketball for the Hurricanes.

In 1966, Barry was selected by the San Francisco Warriors as the second overall pick in the NBA Draft.

During his time with the Warriors, Barry led the team to the NBA Championship in 1975.

In 1976, Barry joined the Houston Rockets, where he played for two seasons before retiring from the NBA in 1980.

After retiring from the NBA, Barry became a successful coach, leading the University of California, Berkeley Golden Bears to the NCAA Tournament in 1993.

Barry is known for his signature underhand free throw shooting style, which he adopted after noticing that players who shot free throws in this manner had higher shooting percentages.

In 1987, Barry was inducted into the Naismith Memorial Basketball Hall of Fame.

Barry is the father of Brent Barry, a former NBA player, and Jon Barry, a former college basketball player and current ESPN analyst.

DID YOU KNOW?

WHO AM I?

Name..

Nickname..

ABOUT ME

Skill

_____

Born

_____

Year Started

_____

INTERESTING FACTS ABOUT ME

 1 _____

 2 _____

 3 _____

Rick Barry was a basketball player who was known for his impressive shooting skills and his ability to lead his team to victory. He was born in Elkins Park, Pennsylvania in 1944 and grew up playing basketball at a young age. Rick was always determined to become the best basketball player he could be, and he worked hard every day to improve his skills.

When Rick was in high school, he was already a standout player on his team. He led his team to the state championship, where they faced off against their biggest rivals, the Lincoln High School Tigers. The game was close, but Rick knew that they had to give it their all if they wanted to come out on top. With just seconds left on the clock, Rick took the ball and drove to the basket, scoring the winning basket and securing the championship for his team.

After high school, Rick decided to pursue his dream of playing college basketball. He received a scholarship to play for the University of Miami, where he quickly became one of the best players on the team. Rick's hard work and dedication paid off, as he helped lead his team to the NCAA Championship in 1966.

After college, Rick decided to pursue a career in professional basketball. He was drafted by the San Francisco Warriors, where he quickly became one of the best players in the league. Rick was known for his ability to score from anywhere on the court, and he was a leader on and off the court. He helped lead the Warriors to the NBA Championship in 1975, and he was named the Finals MVP for his impressive performance.

Rick's success on the court inspired many young children who dreamed of becoming basketball players themselves. They saw Rick as a role model and worked hard to improve their own skills. Many of them even practiced Rick's signature shot, the "granny shot," which was a free throw shot where he shot the ball underhanded.

One young boy named Tim was especially inspired by Rick's story. Tim loved basketball and spent every day practicing his shots and working on his ball handling skills. He dreamed of one day playing in the NBA just like Rick, and he knew that he had to work hard to make that dream a reality.

Tim often thought about Rick's journey to becoming an NBA star, and he used it as motivation to push himself harder. He knew that Rick had faced many challenges and setbacks along the way, but he never let them stop him from achieving his goals. Tim knew that if he wanted to be successful, he had to have the same determination and dedication that Rick had.

As Tim got older, he continued to work hard and improve his skills. He played on his high school team and even led them to the state championship, just like Rick had done. After high school, Tim received a scholarship to play college basketball, and he knew that this was his chance to make his dream of playing in the NBA a reality.

Tim worked harder than ever before, and his hard work paid off. He was named the team's captain and led them to the NCAA Championship, just like Rick had done years before. After college, Tim was drafted by the San Francisco Warriors, and he knew that this was his chance to follow in Rick's footsteps and become an NBA star.

Tim worked hard every day to improve his skills and become the best player he could be. He knew that he had big shoes to fill, but he was determined to make his own mark on the league. And just like Rick, Tim's hard work and dedication paid off. He became one of the top players in the league and helped lead the Warriors to the NBA Championship.

As Tim looked back on his journey, he knew that he couldn't have done it without the inspiration of Rick Barry.

Dennis Rodman

Rodman is a two-time NBA champion, winning titles with the Chicago Bulls in 1996 and 1997.

He is known for his controversial behavior on and off the court, including numerous run-ins with the law and confrontations with teammates and coaches.

Rodman was a member of the "Dream Team" that won gold at the 1992 Summer Olympics in Barcelona.

He is a five-time NBA rebounding champion and was named to the NBA All-Defensive First Team seven times.

Rodman has had several high-profile relationships with celebrities, including Madonna and Carmen Electra.

He has been married and divorced three times.

Rodman has a tattoo of a dragon on his left bicep, which he got in honor of his mother, who was of Chinese descent.

He has a close relationship with North Korean leader Kim Jong-un, and has visited the country several times.

Rodman has appeared on several reality TV shows, including Celebrity Apprentice and The Celebrity Apprentice All-Stars.

He has written several books, including "Bad As I Wanna Be" and "I Should Be Dead By Now".

DID YOU KNOW?

WHO AM I?

Name..

Nickname..

ABOUT ME

Skill

_____

Born

_____

Year Started

_____

INTERESTING FACTS ABOUT ME

 1 _____

 2 _____

 3 _____

Dennis Rodman was a famous basketball player known for his impressive skills on the court and his wild and eccentric personality off the court. But despite his fame and success, Dennis had a rough childhood and had to overcome many challenges to get to where he is today.

Dennis was born in Trenton, New Jersey in 1961. He was the youngest of his siblings and often felt overshadowed by his older brother and sister. Dennis was a quiet and introverted child, and he struggled to make friends at school. He was often teased and bullied by his classmates, which made him feel even more isolated and alone.

But despite his struggles, Dennis found solace in basketball. He was tall and athletic, and he loved the feeling of running up and down the court, the sound of the ball bouncing against the hardwood floor, and the thrill of making a basket. Dennis spent hours practicing his jump shot and working on his ball-handling skills, and he soon became one of the best players on his school's basketball team.

As Dennis grew older, his love for basketball only grew stronger. He worked hard to improve his skills and become the best player he could be. He knew that if he wanted to make it to the NBA, he would have to work harder than anyone else. And that's exactly what he did.

After high school, Dennis received a scholarship to play basketball at Southeastern Oklahoma State University. He excelled on the court, leading his team to the NCAA Division II championship in 1983.

-After college, Dennis was drafted by the Detroit Pistons and became a key member of the team's "Bad Boys" era, helping lead them to back-to-back NBA championships in 1989 and 1990.

But Dennis's success on the court wasn't the only thing that made him famous. He was known for his wild and eccentric personality, with his brightly dyed hair, piercings, and tattoos. He was often seen wearing outrageous outfits and was known for his love of music, art, and fashion.

Despite his fame and success, Dennis faced many challenges and struggles throughout his career. He had a volatile relationship with his teammates and coaches, and he struggled with addiction and mental health issues. But despite these challenges, Dennis never gave up. He worked hard to overcome his struggles and become the best person he could be.

And that's the message that Dennis wants to share with children everywhere: never give up, no matter how hard things may seem. He knows that everyone faces challenges and struggles in life, but it's how we handle them that determines our success and happiness.

Dennis wants children to know that they have the power to overcome any obstacle and achieve their dreams, just like he did. He wants them to know that they are strong and capable, and that they can do anything they set their minds to.

So if you're a child who loves basketball or just wants to be the best you can be, take inspiration from Dennis Rodman. Remember that with hard work, determination, and a little bit of eccentricity, you can achieve anything you want in life.

David Robinson

David Robinson is a retired American professional basketball player who played for the San Antonio Spurs for his entire career.

He was a two-time NBA champion, two-time Olympic gold medalist, and 10-time NBA All-Star.

Robinson is considered one of the best centers in NBA history, with a career average of 21.1 points per game and 10.6 rebounds per game.

He was inducted into the Naismith Memorial Basketball Hall of Fame in 2009.

Before entering the NBA, Robinson attended the United States Naval Academy and served two years in the military.

He was the first player in NBA history to score over 70 points in a single game in the playoffs, which he did in a 2003 game against the Phoenix Suns.

Robinson is known for his philanthropic work, including establishing the Carver Academy, a private school in San Antonio, and the David Robinson Foundation, which provides education and resources to underserved communities.

He is the owner of the San Antonio FC, a professional soccer team in the United Soccer League.

Robinson has a twin brother, Chuck, who is also a former professional basketball player.

In 2007, he was named one of the 50 Greatest Players in NBA History by the league.

DID YOU KNOW?

WHO AM I?

Name..

Nickname..

ABOUT ME

Skill

_____

Born

_____

Year Started

_____

INTERESTING FACTS ABOUT ME

_____

_____

_____

David Robinson was a basketball player who always dreamed of becoming a professional athlete. He was a tall, lanky teenager with a passion for the game and a fierce determination to succeed.

Growing up, David spent hours on the court practicing and perfecting his skills. He was a natural athlete and had a natural ability to shoot, pass, and rebound. But he knew that he couldn't rely on talent alone to achieve his goals. He worked tirelessly to improve his game and became one of the best players in his school.

Despite his talent, David faced many challenges along the way. He was often teased by his peers for being too tall and awkward. He struggled with confidence issues and often doubted his abilities. But he refused to let these setbacks hold him back. He used them as motivation to work even harder and prove his doubters wrong.

After high school, David received a scholarship to play basketball at the Naval Academy. He excelled on the court and quickly became one of the best players in the country. He led his team to numerous victories and was named an All-American player.

After graduation, David was drafted by the San Antonio Spurs and began his professional career. He quickly became one of the best players in the league and led the Spurs to numerous championships. He was named the NBA's Most Valuable Player and became a fan favorite for his impressive skills and sportsmanship.

But David's success on the court was only part of his story. He was also a dedicated husband, father, and philanthropist. He used his platform and influence to make a positive impact in his community and around the world. He supported numerous charities and foundations, and even started his own organization to help underprivileged children.

David's journey to success was far from easy, but he never let his struggles define him. He persevered through adversity and proved that with hard work and determination, anyone can achieve their dreams. He inspired countless young people to pursue their passions and never give up on their goals.

David's story is a testament to the power of perseverance and the importance of never giving up. He faced countless challenges and setbacks along the way, but he never let them hold him back. He used them as motivation to work harder and become the best he could be.

So if you're a young person with a dream, take inspiration from David's story. Remember that with hard work and determination, anything is possible. Don't let your struggles define you, use them as motivation to become the best you can be. Follow your passions, pursue your dreams, and never give up.

Moses Malone

Moses Malone was born in Petersburg, Virginia on March 23, 1955.

He attended Petersburg High School, where he led his team to two consecutive state championships.

Malone was selected by the Portland Trail Blazers in the 1976 NBA Draft, but was immediately traded to the Buffalo Braves.

In his first season with the Braves, he led the league in rebounding, becoming the first player to do so in his rookie season since Bill Russell in 1956.

Malone was a three-time NBA MVP, winning the award in 1979, 1982, and 1983.

He played for several teams during his career, including the Houston Rockets, Philadelphia 76ers, and Atlanta Hawks.

Malone was a 13-time NBA All-Star, and was named to the NBA's 50th Anniversary All-Time Team in 1996.

He was known for his physical style of play and his ability to dominate the boards.

Malone was inducted into the Naismith Memorial Basketball Hall of Fame in 2001.

He passed away on September 13, 2015 at the age of 60 due to cardiac arrest.

DID YOU KNOW?

WHO AM I?

Name..

Nickname..

ABOUT ME

Skill

_____

Born

_____

Year Started

_____

INTERESTING FACTS ABOUT ME

 1 _____

 2 _____

 3 _____

Moses Malone was a basketball player who rose to fame in the 1970s and 1980s. He was known for his powerful and agile playing style, which helped him lead his teams to numerous victories. However, what made Moses truly remarkable was his dedication and determination. He was a man who never gave up, and his hard work and perseverance paid off in the end.

Moses was born in Petersburg, Virginia in 1955. From a young age, he had a love for basketball. He would spend hours practicing his shots and working on his skills. As he got older, his talent on the court began to shine, and he quickly gained recognition for his abilities.

Despite his natural talent, Moses knew that he had to work hard to become a great basketball player. He spent countless hours practicing and honing his skills, and he was always eager to learn more. He was also a team player, always willing to put in the extra effort to help his teammates succeed.

Moses's hard work paid off in high school, where he led his team to numerous victories. He was a dominant force on the court, and his coaches and teammates knew they could always count on him to give his best effort.

After high school, Moses decided to pursue his basketball career at the collegiate level. He chose to attend the University of Maryland, where he continued to excel on the court. He led the team to several conference championships and was named an All-American twice.

After college, Moses was drafted into the NBA by the Portland Trail Blazers. However, he decided to pursue a different opportunity and joined the American Basketball Association (ABA) instead. In the ABA, Moses played for the Spirits of St. Louis, where he quickly became a fan favorite. He led the team to the ABA championship in his first season, and he was named the league's Most Valuable Player.

After the ABA merged with the NBA, Moses joined the Houston Rockets. He quickly became the team's leader and helped guide them to several playoff appearances. He was also named the NBA's Most Valuable Player in 1979, cementing his place as one of the greatest players in the league.

Moses continued to play for the Rockets for several years, but eventually decided to move on to new opportunities. He joined the Philadelphia 76ers in 1982, and helped lead the team to the NBA championship in 1983. This was a crowning achievement for Moses, and he was honored with the Finals MVP award for his outstanding performance.

Throughout his career, Moses remained humble and dedicated to his craft. He was known for his work ethic and his commitment to excellence, and he inspired many young players to pursue their dreams. He was also a role model for children, showing them that hard work and determination can lead to great success.

Moses Malone passed away in 2015, but his legacy lives on. He was a pioneer in the world of basketball and a true inspiration to many. He showed that with hard work and perseverance, anyone can achieve their dreams. So, the next time you feel like giving up, remember Moses Malone and his incredible journey. He proved that anything is possible if you believe in yourself and never give up.

John Stockton

John Stockton was born on March 26, 1962 in Spokane, Washington.

He played college basketball at Gonzaga University before being drafted by the Utah Jazz in 1984.

Stockton played his entire professional career with the Jazz, from 1984-2003.

He is the NBA's all-time leader in assists and steals, with 15,806 assists and 3,265 steals.

Stockton was a 10-time NBA All-Star and was named to the All-NBA First Team twice.

He was inducted into the Naismith Memorial Basketball Hall of Fame in 2009.

Stockton was known for his unassuming personality and leadership on and off the court.

He played in the 1992 and 1996 Summer Olympics as a member of the United States men's national basketball team, winning gold medals in both appearances.

Stockton's number, #12, was retired by the Jazz in 2004.

He is the son of former Washington State Cougars and Idaho Vandals men's basketball coach, Jack Stockton.

DID YOU KNOW?

WHO AM I?

Name..

Nickname..

ABOUT ME

Skill

_____

Born

_____

Year Started

_____

INTERESTING FACTS ABOUT ME

 1 _____

 2 _____

 3 _____

John Stockton was a professional basketball player who played for the Utah Jazz for his entire career. He was known for his exceptional ball handling skills, his ability to set up his teammates, and his defensive prowess. Stockton was a ten-time NBA All-Star and was inducted into the Basketball Hall of Fame in 2009.

Despite his accolades and success, Stockton never let it get to his head. He remained humble and worked hard every day to improve his game. He always put the team first and was a true leader on and off the court.

One of the most inspiring stories about John Stockton was when he led his high school basketball team to a state championship. Stockton was only a junior at the time, but he had already established himself as one of the best players in the state. He had a natural talent for the game and worked tirelessly to improve his skills.

As the team's captain, Stockton took it upon himself to lead the team to victory. He was a fierce competitor, but he also knew how to motivate and encourage his teammates. He knew that they were all in it together and that they needed to work as a team to achieve their goals.

In the championship game, Stockton led his team to a comeback victory with a clutch three-pointer in the final seconds. His teammates mobbed him on the court, and the fans erupted in cheers. It was a moment that Stockton would never forget, and it taught him the importance of teamwork and leadership.

After high school, Stockton decided to attend Gonzaga University, where he played college basketball. He had a successful career at Gonzaga, but it was his time with the Jazz that really put him on the map.

Stockton joined the Jazz in 1984, and he quickly became one of the team's top players. He and his teammate, Karl Malone, formed one of the most dynamic duos in NBA history. Together, they led the Jazz to the playoffs every year and made it to the NBA Finals twice.

Stockton was known for his unselfish play and his ability to set up his teammates. He was always looking for the open man and never hesitated to pass the ball. He was also a tenacious defender and was known for his ability to steal the ball from opponents.

Despite his success on the court, Stockton remained humble and never let it go to his head. He always put the team first and was a true leader in the locker room. He was the ultimate role model for his teammates, and they always looked up to him.

One of the things that made Stockton such an inspiration was his work ethic. He was always the first one at practice and the last one to leave. He knew that hard work and dedication were the keys to success, and he instilled those values in his teammates.

Stockton's commitment to hard work and teamwork paid off in the form of numerous accolades and achievements. He was a ten-time NBA All-Star, and he was inducted into the Basketball Hall of Fame in 2009. He was also named to the NBA's 50th Anniversary All-Time Team and was named one of the 100 Greatest Players in NBA History.

Despite all of his accolades and achievements, Stockton remained humble and never let it go to his head. He knew that he was fortunate to have had the opportunity to play professional basketball and he never took it for granted.

Stockton retired from the NBA in 2003, but his impact on the game and his teammates lived on. He left a lasting legacy as a leader and a role model, and he inspired countless young players to pursue their dreams and work hard to achieve their goals.

Clyde Drexler

Clyde Drexler was born on June 22, 1962, in New Orleans, Louisiana.

He attended the University of Houston, where he played college basketball for the Cougars.

Drexler was drafted by the Portland Trail Blazers with the 14th overall pick in the 1983 NBA Draft.

He played for the Blazers for over a decade, leading the team to the NBA Finals in 1990 and 1992.

Drexler was a 10-time NBA All-Star and was named to the All-NBA First Team in 1992.

He won an Olympic gold medal in 1992 as a member of the United States Olympic basketball team.

In 1995, Drexler was traded to the Houston Rockets, where he played alongside Hakeem Olajuwon and won an NBA championship in 1995.

He retired from the NBA in 1998 after 15 seasons in the league.

Drexler was inducted into the Naismith Memorial Basketball Hall of Fame in 2004.

After his playing career, Drexler became a coach and broadcaster, working for the Rockets and ESPN.

DID YOU KNOW?

WHO AM I?

Name..

Nickname..

ABOUT ME

Skill

_____

Born

_____

Year Started

_____

INTERESTING FACTS ABOUT ME

1 _____

2 _____

3 _____

Clyde Drexler was a basketball player who inspired many children to follow their dreams and work hard to achieve their goals. He was born on June 22, 1962, in New Orleans, Louisiana, and grew up in Houston, Texas.

From a young age, Clyde had a passion for basketball. He played on his school's team and spent hours practicing his skills in the park with his friends. Despite facing challenges and setbacks, Clyde never gave up on his dream of becoming a professional basketball player.

One day, while playing in a local tournament, Clyde caught the attention of a college coach who offered him a scholarship to play for the University of Houston. Clyde jumped at the opportunity and worked hard to improve his game. He led the Cougars to the NCAA Championship game in 1983, where they lost to North Carolina State.

After college, Clyde was drafted by the Portland Trail Blazers and quickly became a star player. He helped lead the team to the NBA Finals in 1990, where they lost to the Detroit Pistons. However, Clyde's determination and hard work paid off in 1992 when he was a part of the Dream Team that won the gold medal at the Summer Olympics in Barcelona.

Clyde's success on the court inspired many children to pursue their dreams and work hard to achieve their goals. He became a role model for young basketball players and showed them that with hard work and dedication, anything is possible.

Despite facing challenges and setbacks, Clyde never gave up on his dream of becoming a professional basketball player. He faced criticism and doubters who said he couldn't make it to the top, but Clyde never let that discourage him. He used it as motivation to work even harder and prove them wrong.

Clyde's determination and perseverance paid off when he was named the NBA All-Star Game Most Valuable Player in 1992. He was also inducted into the Basketball Hall of Fame in 2004, cementing his place as one of the greatest basketball players of all time.

In addition to his success on the court, Clyde was also a great role model off the court. He was known for his charitable work and his commitment to giving back to his community. He worked with organizations that provided resources and support for underprivileged children, helping to improve their lives and provide them with opportunities for a better future.

Clyde's story is an inspiration to children everywhere, showing them that with hard work and determination, they can overcome any obstacle and achieve their dreams. He proved that no matter where you come from or what challenges you face, you have the power to create your own path and succeed.

So if you're a child who has a dream, take Clyde Drexler as your inspiration and never give up. Work hard, stay determined, and you too can achieve greatness. Remember, anything is possible if you put your mind to it.

Patrick Ewing

Patrick Ewing was born in Kingston, Jamaica and immigrated to the United States at a young age.

Ewing attended Georgetown University, where he played college basketball under coach John Thompson Jr.

Ewing was a three-time All-American at Georgetown and led the team to the NCAA Championship in 1984.

Ewing was the first overall pick in the 1985 NBA Draft, chosen by the New York Knicks.

Ewing played for the Knicks for 15 seasons, leading the team to the NBA Finals in 1994 and 1999.

Ewing was a 11-time NBA All-Star and was inducted into the Naismith Memorial Basketball Hall of Fame in 2008.

Ewing was known for his dominant post presence and shot blocking ability, leading the league in blocks three times.

Ewing won a gold medal with the U.S. Olympic basketball team in 1984 and 1992.

After retiring as a player, Ewing became a coach and has served as an assistant coach for multiple NBA teams.

Ewing has also worked as a television analyst for ESPN and has a successful sneaker line with Fila.

Patrick Ewing

DID YOU KNOW?

WHO AM I?

Name..

Nickname..

ABOUT ME

Skill

_____

Born

_____

Year Started

_____

INTERESTING FACTS ABOUT ME

1 _____

2 _____

3 _____

Patrick Ewing was a legendary basketball player who inspired countless young athletes to pursue their dreams. His hard work and dedication on the court made him one of the most respected players in the game, and his impact on the sport is still felt today.

Growing up in Jamaica, Patrick had a natural talent for basketball. He was tall and athletic, with a strong desire to succeed. When he was just a teenager, he moved to the United States to attend college and pursue his dreams of becoming a professional basketball player.

At Georgetown University, Patrick quickly made a name for himself. He was a dominant force on the court, leading the team to the NCAA Championship in 1984. His performance earned him the title of Most Outstanding Player, and he became a household name in the world of college basketball.

After college, Patrick was drafted by the New York Knicks, where he spent most of his professional career. He quickly became a fan favorite, with his powerful dunks and fierce determination on the court. He led the Knicks to the NBA Finals on multiple occasions, but unfortunately, they were never able to win the championship.

Despite the disappointment of not winning a championship, Patrick remained a role model for young athletes everywhere. He was known for his work ethic and his dedication to the game, and he inspired many young players to strive for greatness.

One of those young players was a young boy named Tim. Tim was a huge basketball fan, and he looked up to Patrick as a hero. He would often watch Patrick's games on TV, and he dreamed of one day becoming a professional basketball player just like him.

Tim practiced every day, working tirelessly to improve his skills. He spent hours in the gym, shooting baskets and perfecting his moves. And every time he stepped on the court, he gave it his all, just like Patrick did.

One day, Tim had the opportunity to meet Patrick in person. He was at a basketball camp where Patrick was a guest speaker, and he was beyond excited to finally meet his hero.

When Patrick arrived, Tim couldn't believe how tall and imposing he was. But as soon as Patrick spoke, Tim was struck by how kind and humble he was. He talked about the importance of hard work and dedication, and he encouraged the young players to always give their best effort.

Tim was inspired by Patrick's words, and he knew that he had to work even harder to reach his goals. He left the camp with a renewed sense of determination and a strong desire to succeed.

Over the next few years, Tim continued to work hard and improve his game. He practiced every day, and he never let setbacks discourage him. He was always looking for ways to get better, just like Patrick did.

Finally, after years of hard work, Tim's dream became a reality. He was recruited to play college basketball at Georgetown University, just like Patrick did. And when he stepped on the court for the first time, he knew that all of his hard work had paid off.

As he played in college, Tim remembered the lessons that Patrick had taught him. He worked hard every day, and he never gave up. And eventually, he became one of the best players in the country, just like Patrick had been.

When Tim graduated from college, he was drafted by the New York Knicks, just like Patrick had been. And as he took the court for the first time, he knew that he was following in the footsteps of his hero.

Grant Hill

Grant Hill attended Duke University where he played college basketball and earned a degree in political science.

Hill was a member of the United States Olympic team that won a gold medal at the 1996 Atlanta Olympics.

Hill was selected as the third overall pick in the NBA Draft by the Detroit Pistons in 1994.

During his professional career, Hill played for the Pistons, Orlando Magic, Phoenix Suns, and Los Angeles Clippers.

Hill was a seven-time NBA All-Star and was named to the All-NBA Second Team three times.

Hill is known for his versatility on the court, as he was able to play multiple positions and contribute to his team in various ways.

In 2000, Hill won the NBA Sportsmanship Award, which is given annually to the player who exemplifies the ideals of sportsmanship on the court.

Hill suffered numerous injuries during his career, which ultimately led to his retirement in 2013.

Hill is a member of the Naismith Memorial Basketball Hall of Fame, having been inducted in 2018.

In addition to his basketball career, Hill has also pursued a successful business career, investing in real estate and serving on the board of directors for several companies.

Grant Hill

DID YOU KNOW?

WHO AM I?

Name..

Nickname..

ABOUT ME

Skill

Born

Year Started

INTERESTING FACTS ABOUT ME

1 _____
_____

2 _____
_____

3 _____
_____

Once upon a time, there was a young boy named Grant Hill who loved to play basketball. He spent every waking moment practicing his jump shot and dribbling skills, dreaming of one day becoming a professional basketball player.

As he grew older, Grant worked hard to hone his skills and became one of the best players in his high school team. He was tall, fast, and had a natural talent for the game. His coaches and teammates knew he had the potential to go far.

After graduating from high school, Grant received a scholarship to attend Duke University, where he played for the Blue Devils basketball team. He quickly became a star player, leading the team to the NCAA Championship and earning numerous accolades for his outstanding performance on the court.

After college, Grant was drafted by the Detroit Pistons, where he became a key member of the team and helped lead them to the NBA Finals. He was known for his strong work ethic and leadership abilities, and was soon named the team captain.

Despite his success on the court, Grant faced many challenges in his career. He suffered numerous injuries that kept him off the court for extended periods of time, and at times, it seemed like his dream of becoming a professional basketball player was slipping away.

But Grant never gave up. He worked tirelessly to rehabilitate his injuries and get back on the court, and eventually, he was able to return to top form.

He became one of the best players in the league, earning numerous All-Star selections and being named to the All-NBA team.

But Grant's greatest achievement came off the court. He became a role model for young basketball players everywhere, showing them that hard work and determination can overcome any obstacle. He started a charitable foundation to help underprivileged youth, and became known for his generosity and kindness.

One day, a group of young basketball players from a local Boys and Girls Club approached Grant and asked him for some advice on how to become a successful basketball player. Grant took the time to talk to the kids and share his experiences with them, telling them about the importance of hard work, dedication, and perseverance.

"If you really want to achieve your dreams, you have to be willing to put in the work," he told them. "There will be times when you want to give up, but you can't let that happen. You have to keep pushing forward, no matter how hard it gets. That's the only way to succeed."

The kids listened intently to Grant's words, and were inspired by his story. They knew that if Grant could overcome his injuries and become a top player, they could do it too. They vowed to work hard and never give up on their dreams, just like Grant did.

And as they grew older and continued to play basketball, they never forgot the lessons they learned from Grant Hill. They became hardworking, dedicated players, and many of them went on to have successful careers in the sport.

So remember, kids, if you want to achieve your dreams, don't be afraid to work hard and never give up. With determination and perseverance, you can overcome any obstacle and reach your goals, just like Grant Hill did.

Made in the USA
Las Vegas, NV
02 March 2023

68383569R00077